MW01232738

MICHIGAN

Where Have You Gone?

JIM CNOCKAERT

WWW.SPORTSPUBLISHINGLLC.COM

Director of production: Susan M. Moyer
Acquisitions editor: Mike Pearson
Project manager: Jim Henehan
Developmental editor: Kipp Wilfong
Dust jacket design and imaging: Kenneth J. O'Brien
Copy editor: Cynthia L. McNew
Photo editor: Erin Linden-Levy
Marketing manager: Jonathan Patterson

Insert photos courtesy of individuals photographed except where noted.

Interior photos courtesy of University of Michigan Sports Information except where noted.

ISBN: 1-58261-771-6

Printed in the United States.

To Christine, my best friend and partner for life. Your abiding love, unwavering support and enthusiastic encouragement helped me to get through a most difficult time in my life. Thank you for believing in me.

CONTENTS

INTRODUCTION

The history of University of Michigan football has been well documented. No college program has more wins, plays in a bigger stadium or features a more recognized icon, the famed winged helmet. The school's fight song, "The Victors," is regarded as one of the finest ever written. In 124 seasons, Michigan has won 41 Big Ten championships and 11 national titles, and has produced three Heisman Trophy winners. The program's current bowl streak stands at 29 seasons and counting. The Wolverines have not had a losing season since Bo Schembechler took over as head coach in 1969, while most other programs with similar history and tradition have gone through some sort of downturn, even if just momentary.

Why has Michigan been so successful for so long? The obvious reason is tradition. Fielding H. Yost, the coach credited with establishing Michigan's winning ways, once said that Michigan's place was above all others. He put the program there, and his successors, from Harry Kipke to Fritz Crisler to Bo Schembechler to Lloyd Carr, have kept it there. Crisler once said that Michigan's tradition couldn't be bottled or bought at the corner store, but that it was there to sustain the program and its players through difficult times. Simply put, Michigan teams believe they will win because that is what Michigan teams historically have done.

When other coaches would ask Yost whether there was a secret to creating tradition, he would reply: "You don't put morale on like a coat. You build it day by day." He could just as easily have said: You build it with players of great courage and character, who love their university and its football program, who put team goals ahead of their own.

Michigan has been winning with players like that since 1879, when captain Dave DeTar kicked a goal to beat Racine College, 1-0, in the first

Michigan football game ever played. It's important to understand this, because Michigan tradition is about much more than winning football games. It is about every player who gave all he had for something bigger than himself. What was the reward for doing that? Each player, in his own way, helped to make history.

This book chronicles some of that history by recounting the stories of 50 former Michigan players. Admittedly, considering the number of young men who have played even a down for the Wolverines through parts of three centuries, it is a tiny sampling. But listening to the stories of these men, whose ages range from 88 to 25, it became clear that, while particulars vary, their experiences are remarkably similar.

With notable exceptions, they were the best players on their high school teams and recruited by many of the top college programs in the country. They arrived in Ann Arbor expecting to be superstars, only to discover there were 100 or more other young men with the same goal.

Some, like Chuck Ortmann and Rob Renes, had dreamed all their lives that they would one day play for the Wolverines. Others, like Jim Betts and Garvie Craw, felt an immediate bond with the veteran players and the coaches when they first met them. Others, like Ron Johnson and Tripp Welborne, who visited a number of colleges and did much soul-searching, decided that Michigan offered just the right combination of academic and athletic excellence. Still others, like Hercules Renda and J.D. Carlson, believe they were lucky that Michigan wanted them.

Each of them faced some sort of adversity once they were on the team. Some lost playing time or careers to injury. Some changed positions for the sake of the team. Some had ongoing disagreements with their coaches. Some believed they were unfairly treated. Some would have personal struggles later in life. Each would fall back on the lessons he learned in practices and in games.

Not one of them would trade their Michigan experience, because they recognize what it meant to them. They arrived in Ann Arbor as boys, and graduated as men. They learned to pull together for the sake of a common goal, even if that meant giving up some of their own goals. Their teammates became—and still are—their best friends. Ultimately, they learned that the character of a person isn't measured by what happens to him, but by how he reacts to those circumstances.

Dick Vidmer's story is worth noting. He sustained a serious injury early in his college career that limited some of his marvelous athletic talents, but he came back to become the Wolverines' starting quarterback for a time in the mid-1960s. He was a brilliant student. Afflicted by multiple sclerosis, he is now a quadriplegic who cannot care for himself and must spend his waking hours in a wheelchair. But he has remarkable courage and insight. He sees his disease, not as a curse, but as a blessing. He would not change anything about his life, he says, because every experience has been meaningful. It is an attitude he developed, in part, during his years at Michigan.

Through all of it, Vidmer remains fiercely loyal to his alma mater and, in particular, to its football program. "I can't imagine a better place to experience college football than Michigan," he said. "You can't buy an experience like that. You can't put too high a value on it."

It is a sentiment the other 49 men in this book echo.

DICK BALZHISER

If anyone epitomized the term "student-athlete" during his undergraduate years at Michigan, it was Dick Balzhiser.

He was the "spinning fullback" (the equivalent of an option quarterback) in Coach Bennie Oosterbaan's intricate and deceptive single-wing offense from 1952-53. He also carried slightly less than a 4.0 grade-point average in chemical engineering.

Add this to that workload: Balzhiser married his high school sweetheart, Christine, in 1951, and the couple soon was raising two babies. Because there were no athletic scholarships then, Balzhiser supported his young family by doing odd jobs, many provided by the athletic department. Those included scraping the ice and selling hot dogs at Michigan hockey games, stocking shelves at a local bookstore and dusting pews at the Lutheran church the family attended. "There were no breaks for football players, and I was paying out-of-state tuition," he said. "I'd take on anything that would make me a little money."

In 1952, he became the first Michigan football player to earn first-team academic All-America honors. Two years later he was awarded the Big Ten Medal of Honor because of his proficiency on the football field and in the classroom.

Balzhiser grew up in Wheaton, Illinois, the home of former University of Illinois star Red Grange, but he had little interest in play-

DICK BALZHISER
Michigan letterman: 1952-1953

Position: Fullback **Number:** 38 **Hometown:** Wheaton, Illinois

Academic All-American, 1952
Career rushing: 129 carries, 492 yards, 3 TDs
Top game: 21 carries, 53 yards, 2 TDs vs. Minnesota, 1952

ing for the Fighting Illini. In an era when many high school and college programs were using a standard single wing or changing to the new T-formation, Wheaton's single wing was modeled after the one used by Michigan, and it featured Balzhiser as the "spinning fullback." No other high school team used that offense. Michigan coach Bennie Oosterbaan eagerly recruited Balzhiser because of his experience at the Wolverines' key offensive position.

In the single wing, no player lines up under the center, who could snap the ball to any one of the four players in the backfield. Most snaps went to the fullback, who after spinning to disguise the nature and direction of the play, could hand the ball off to one of his backfield mates, keep it and run himself, or (on rare occasions) pass the ball. "It had the advantage in that it was hard to prepare for because no one else used it," he said.

Football taught Balzhiser a lot about discipline, preparation and time management, which was critical in helping him to juggle all the demands on his time during his undergraduate years. He admits he was fortunate in one respect: Oosterbaan believed that class work came first, not football, so Balzhiser was allowed to come late to practice on the days when he had afternoon science lab classes. "I never missed a lab," he said.

Balzhiser saved what he considers to be his best game for last. He was the Wolverines' second-leading rusher—he carried 11 times for 40 yards and a touchdown—in a 20-0 win against Ohio State at Michigan Stadium. "It was always a pleasure to beat Woody, because in those days we didn't do it too often," he said. A year earlier in Columbus, Balzhiser had been Michigan's leading rusher (10 carries, 70 yards) in a 27-7 loss to the Buckeyes.

After earning his bachelor's degree in chemical engineering, Balzhiser remained at Michigan to earn a master's in nuclear engineering and a Ph.D. in chemical engineering. He joined the Michigan faculty in 1961, and was named chairman of the chemical engineering department in 1971.

But Balzhiser also was interested in public service. He was elected to the Ann Arbor city council in the 1960s. He earned a White House fellowship in 1967, and spent a year in Washington, D.C., working for Secretary of Defense Robert McNamara. Balzhiser returned to the nation's capital in 1971 to spend two years under President Richard Nixon in the Office of Science and Technology, where he oversaw energy, environment and natural resources.

During that second Washington stint, he met Chauncey Starr, the founder of the Electric Power Research Institute. Starr persuaded

Balzhiser to join his organization, and the family moved to southern California in 1973. At EPRI, he started as director of the Fossil Fuel and Advanced Systems Division. He became the vice president of research and development in 1979, and he assumed the company's presidency in 1988. At age 72, he is now semi-retired, though he has provided expert information on two recent studies commissioned by the White House on science and technology.

Though his first love was football, Balzhiser's job experience with the Michigan hockey program would be a greater influence on his children. He didn't play hockey, but he loved to watch it, so each winter he created an ice rink in the backyard where his four children learned to skate. His two sons eventually played hockey at Yale University; his daughters became competitive figure skaters.

Five decades after earning academic All-America honors, Balzhiser was honored yet again: In 2002, he was named by the College Sports Information Directors of America to the Academic All-America Hall of Fame for his "accomplishments in academics, athletics, professional career and community service."

"That award was a real surprise," he said. "(At the banquet in New York City), I had the opportunity to talk with a number of distinguished athletes who had been good academicians, and I realized how lucky I was to attend Michigan, an academically oriented school where the programs were challenging. And of all the football teams I was aware of, Michigan was blessed with good people who deserved to be on campus."

Where Have You Gone?

BRAD BATES

I t was hot in Coach Bo Schembechler's office and Brad Bates was already sweating because he was in the presence of the legendary Michigan coach, but he refused to remove the puffy down jacket he was wearing. The jacket made him appear to be bigger, which was reassuring, because Bates was afraid Schembechler would tell him he was too small to play big-time college football.

Bates was a two-sport star at Port Huron (Michigan) Northern High School, but no big schools recruited him. Determined to play Division I football, Bates had his father, Jim, the Northern football coach, arrange meetings with the coaching staffs at Michigan State and Michigan. He met with an MSU graduate assistant who told him he could try out for the team as soon as classes started. It might have been because his father was a former Michigan player, but Schembechler took time out from a spring staff meeting to meet with the Bates. By the time the conversation was over, Bates was hooked. He walked on at Michigan.

The attrition rate among walk-ons in most Division I programs is high because those players get few perks and even less playing time compared to their scholarship classmates. Bates was the only one of the nine walk-ons in his class who lasted four seasons, but he was much more than a survivor. He so impressed Michigan coaches that he became a reg-

Photo courtesy of Bob Kalmbach, University of Michigan

BRAD BATES
Michigan letterman: 1980

Position: Defensive back **Number:** 12
Hometown: Port Huron, Michigan

Career defense: 6 tackles
Top game: 1 interception vs. Northwestern, 1979

ular on special teams his senior season, 1980, when he contributed to a Big Ten championship run and Schembechler's first Rose Bowl victory.

Ironically, Bates, the kid who worried he wasn't big enough to play at Michigan, made that big impression with his physical attributes. Former teammates say Bates was the best-conditioned athlete with whom they'd ever played, and it was no accident. Knowing he needed to do something to catch the coaches' attention, he dominated the series of summer conditioning tests every Michigan football player was required to pass before training camp.

"It was almost like a decathlon of strength and conditioning, so whatever the tests were, that's what I trained for—to make an impression on the coaches," he said. "I'm a coach's kid, and I understood football. I knew I couldn't just finish second or third. If I wanted to get the coaches to remember who I was, I had to do very, very well, and that's what I tried to do. I felt that would give me opportunities I wouldn't get otherwise."

Bates, who had been a quarterback in high school, tried a number of positions his freshman season, 1977, while playing on the demonstration teams. He earned some meaningful practice time after moving to defensive back in the spring, but he was back on the demonstrations teams in the fall because of the arrival of Keith Bostic. Bates's intensity, conditioning and hard work finally paid off at the end of his junior season, when he earned a spot on the travel team as a special teams player.

His timing could not have been much better. During Bates's junior season, the punt team suffered a series of breakdowns that proved costly in games, so Schembechler took over responsibility for that unit the following spring. In fact, there was a renewed emphasis on all special teams that spring, which raised the stature of any player who participated on those units. "The guys on the punt team weren't necessarily starters, but they took great pride in what they did," said Bates, who was the "up" back in punt formation. "It was a great honor to be on that squad, and it expanded to the others. Once you made it, you worked hard to improve your performance because you had guys nipping at your heels the whole time. Once I got in there, I didn't want to lose my job."

Bates played well against Michigan State and Minnesota during his senior season, and the special teams played a key role in a 9-3 win at Ohio State that clinched the Big Ten championship.

The moment Bates remembers most from that season came at the conclusion of the Rose Bowl, as the Wolverines celebrated a 23-6 win against Washington. "I was walking off the field with George Lilja, and he said, 'Let's turn around for a Kodak moment,'" Bates recalled. "You could see that big orange backdrop against the mountains. This was Bo's first bowl victory. Your teammates are all walking around you. It is very, very clear in my mind. Winning it for Bo was what really made it special."

With degrees in English and physical education, Bates planned to follow his father's footsteps into teaching, but he changed his mind when Schembechler offered him a job as a graduate assistant. Bates spent much of that time working with Mike Gittleson, the program's strength and conditioning coach. When assistant Bill McCartney left to become the head coach at Colorado, he asked Bates to join him as the Buffaloes' strength coach. Three years later, he took a similar job at Vanderbilt. He left football to move into Vanderbilt's athletic administration at Vanderbilt, and he eventually became a senior associate director.

Not long after earning a doctorate in higher curriculum from Vanderbilt, Bates was considered for the Michigan athletic director opening in the winter of 2000, but university President Lee Bollinger eventually appointed Ann Arbor businessman Bill Martin to the position. "That was an interesting experience, because I had never interviewed for a job in my life," Bates said. "Now I was in a room with a dozen people at my alma mater. It was pretty exciting."

Bates was hired as athletic director at Miami University in Oxford, Ohio, in 2002. "If you're a coach's son and you're at the Cradle of Coaches, imagine how much fun that is," he said. "As a regular deal, I get to talk to (Ara) Parseghian, Schembechler, (Bill) Mallory, (John) Pont, as well as many others. That's an amazing laundry list of people who have gone through here."

Bates and his wife, Michele, celebrated their 21st anniversary last summer. They have no children, though Bates jokes that they have 522 18- to 23-year-olds—the Miami athletes.

"In the context of my life, the most important decision I ever made was going to Michigan and playing football there," he said. "The experiences I had and the lessons I learned influence what I am doing today. And in terms of my (Michigan) coaches, there probably isn't a day that goes by that I don't use something I learned from that group."

Where Have You Gone?

GORDON BELL

Gordy Bell does not begrudge Ohio State's Archie Griffin his two Heisman Trophies, but he believes he was at least as good as Griffin, if not better.

The statistics from their head-to-head meetings in 1974 and 1975 bear this out. It was pretty much a wash when he and Griffin faced each other in Ohio Stadium in '74: Each carried 25 times; Bell finished with 108 yards, and Griffin gained 111. It was a much different story their senior seasons at Michigan Stadium: Bell gained 124 yards on 21 carries; Griffin was held to 46 yards on 19 tries. In fact, Griffin was not the Big Ten's leading rusher in either of the two seasons he won the Heisman. Bell averaged 132.9 yards a game to lead the conference in 1975, but he wound up eighth in the Heisman voting. Wisconsin's Billy Marek was the conference rushing leader in 1974.

"Those two games against Ohio State were my biggest, and I consider the second game a personal victory," Bell said. "I outrushed Archie, but he had a great public relations guy in (Coach) Woody Hayes. If it had been me and I had won the Heisman, I would have said it was great. But he wasn't the best player in the conference, so how can he be the best player in the country?"

GORDON BELL
Michigan letterman: 1973-1975

Position: Tailback **Number:** 5
Hometown: Troy, Ohio

All-Big Ten, 1975
Career rushing: 535 carries, 2,902 yards, 28 TDs
Top game: 31 carries, 174 yards, 2 TDs at Minnesota, 1975

But Bell admits he takes only so much consolation in such individual triumphs. He might have been the better running back, but the Buckeyes won both games—12-10 in 1974 and 21-14 in 1975—and earned trips to the Rose Bowl.

There was no team that Bell, a native of Troy, Ohio, wanted to beat more than Ohio State. His father was a dyed-in-the-wool Buckeyes fan, and Bell had attended games at Ohio Stadium since he was six years old. The game-day routine never varied: He and his father ate breakfast at the student union; watched touch football games on the Diag; listened to the marching band perform at St. John Arena; and, finally, got to the stadium in time to watch the teams warm up. Bell was so sick of it that, by the time he was 13 years old, he was rooting against the Buckeyes. He'd already made up his mind: He would never play for Ohio State.

Heading into his senior season, Bell was regarded as one of the top football prospects in Ohio. He was interested in Michigan State, which had been the Big Ten's dominant team in the mid-1960s, but he became a Michigan fan in 1971 after he watched the Wolverines defeat Ohio State at Michigan Stadium. Michigan assistant Gary Moeller was a regular visitor after that, but Bell's father made certain he was never home when a Michigan coach stopped by. "Once I made the decision to go to Michigan, my dad became a staunch fan," Bell said. "On the morning of home games, he'd be outside the Campus Inn (where the team stayed in Ann Arbor), and he'd greet Bo and the players as we boarded the busses to go to the stadium. He became the official bus greeter."

Though he liked Michigan best, Bell nearly went elsewhere to play. He and a teammate had agreed to go to the same college, and because both were Catholic, they chose Notre Dame. His teammate later changed his mind and committed to Florida. Bell had no interest in going there, so he made a last-minute call to Coach Bo Schembechler to find out if Michigan had any scholarships left. At first, Schembechler said there were none left. He called Bell a day later to say he'd found one.

At 5-9, 170 pounds, Bell was a finesse runner rather than a power back, but he loved to run between the tackles. "I could pick the holes really well, and I'd get in and get out," he said. "We practiced so many situations every day in practice that by the end of the week, you knew where the holes would be. Bo was always live at the line. It was full force, full contact at the point of attack all the time. By the end of the week, you'd played the game."

Bell hit his stride as Michigan's featured tailback midway through his junior season (1974), when he ran for 134 yards against Minnesota. He ran for more than 100 yards in each of the Wolverines' remaining four games that season, and he rushed for 100 yards in all but two of Michigan's 12 games in 1975. He ran for a career-high 210 yards in the 1975 season opener at Wisconsin. He finished his senior season with 1,390 yards and 13 touchdowns. In his four-year career, he ran for 2,902 yards and 28 touchdowns.

Before the 1975 season, only the Big Ten champion (or runner-up under the conference's no-repeat rule) could play in a bowl game. That kept three outstanding Michigan teams home during the holidays from 1972-74. Finally in 1975, the Big Ten opened the door to other conference teams, and Michigan accepted an invitation to play third-ranked Oklahoma in the Orange Bowl.

Against a Sooners defense led by the Selmon brothers, Bell managed just 53 yards and a touchdown on 18 carries. Oklahoma prevailed, 14-6. "That was a hard-fought game," he recalled. "Oklahoma really brought it to you. I never felt so sore after a game. My teammates went out after the game, but I had to go back to the hotel to lay down. My arms and legs felt like pincushions."

Bell was the first Michigan player taken in the 1976 NFL Draft. The New York Giants selected him in the fourth round. He played two seasons with the Giants, and then played eight weeks with Ottawa of the Canadian Football League before returning to the NFL to finish the season—and his career—with the St. Louis Cardinals.

He returned to Ohio and opened a BBQ restaurant in Dayton. He then moved to Detroit, where he sold radio advertising for 10 years. Now 51, he has spent the last nine years in Chicago, working much of that time as a senior sales executive for WGCI radio.

Bell met his wife, Nancy, when he lived in Dayton, and the two have been married for 11 years. The couple has three children: Marjory, 8; Evan, 6; and, Adam, 2.

Even now, he says with a chuckle, he cannot escape the shadow of the Buckeyes. His wife is an Ohio State graduate.

Where Have You Gone?

JIM BETTS

Jim Betts was a man of many positions during his Michigan football career. He played quarterback his freshman season, but as a sophomore he switched to running back and then to wide receiver. Bo Schembechler, who'd tried to recruited Betts to play quarterback while he was coach at Miami of Ohio, moved Betts back to that position when he took over at Michigan in 1969. Unhappy solely in a reserve role, Betts convinced Schembechler to allow him to move to safety for his senior season while he continued to be the backup at quarterback.

"I was just looking for a way to get on the field," he said.

Betts grins as he recalls the meeting before his senior season during which he *informed* Schembechler that he planned to switch to defense. He had already discussed the move with assistant coach Dick Hunter, who was eager to add Betts to a secondary that had been depleted by graduation. "I went to Bo, and he said: 'You don't tell me what to do. You're my back-up quarterback,'" Betts said. "I told him I didn't want to sit the bench all year, and I told him I could do both. He demanded to know how I was going to do that. I told him the quarterback job wasn't all that tough. We worked it out." Betts attended quarterback meetings in the morning and defensive backfield meetings in the afternoon, and he played on defense in the first part of practice and offense in the sec-

JIM BETTS
Michigan letterman: 1968-1970

Position: Defensive back **Number:** 23
Hometown: Cleveland, Ohio

Career defense: 45 tackles, 4 pass breakups, 2 fumble recoveries, 2 interceptions **Top game:** 14 tackles, 1 interception at Ohio State, 1970

ond part. "I'd played both ways in high school, so I didn't think it was that big a deal," he said.

That wasn't the first time Betts and a Michigan coach didn't see eye to eye on something, nor would it be the last.

In the spring of 1969, an angry Schembechler kicked Betts in the rear end during a practice after he'd made a series of mistakes trying to quarterback the offense. Betts insisted that Schembechler leave a staff meeting the following morning so he could tell the coach that "if God had intended for me to have a foot in my rear end, he would have put one there."

In the fourth quarter of a 45-7 win against Washington that season, Schembechler instructed Betts and the second-team offense to run out the clock. Betts intended to do just that, but on an option run-pass play, he spied receiver Billy Harris wide open down the field. Betts' instincts kicked in, and he fired a perfect pass for a touchdown. An angry Schembechler met Betts when he got to the sideline. "He told us that he had put us out there to run out the clock, not run up the score," he said. "Bo pulled us out. (Reggie) McKenzie and a bunch of the linemen were mad at me. They wanted to get some playing time."

The Sunday after a 39-13 homecoming win against Minnesota in 1970, Betts was 10 minutes late to the afternoon team meeting because he'd had to first pick up a teammate. After yelling at Betts for a minute or two, Schembechler began to announce the individual champion awards from the previous day's game. When he came to the defensive star, he noted that the player had scored 100 percent on all of his assignments and tackles. Then Schembechler realized about whom he was talking—Betts—and he hesitated momentarily to announce his name. Finally, he called Betts to the front of the room and handed him the small trophy each champion received. "Then he turned his back on me," Betts recalled.

Betts was one of two Division I prospects—the other was Larry Celina, who wound up at Ohio State—to come out of Cleveland Benedictine High School in 1967. Benedictine coach Augie Bossu, a former University of Notre Dame player, did not allow college coaches to contact his players until the conclusion of their senior seasons. When the team returned to school after its season finale, Bossu handed both Betts and Celina two boxes of letters from recruiters he had kept for them. The two players went into the gym, dumped the letters on the floor and began to sort through the piles. There were letters from more than 100 schools, ranging from the Big Ten and Mid-American conferences to

Atlantic Coast and Pac-8 conferences, to seemingly every conference in between. "It was pretty overwhelming," he said.

Suddenly, recruiters began to hound the two players. Bossu gave his players some guidelines they could use to narrow their choices. "We looked at the academic side, the athletic side, the potential to play right away, what the college would do for you once you graduated, and whether we'd fit in on campus," he said. Many schools wanted Betts to come in as a defensive back, and he eliminated them from consideration. Michigan assistant coach Don James assured Betts he'd play quarterback, but he was realistic about Betts's opportunities. He was one of four quarterbacks in his class. Each of them was given a half to play in one of the freshman team's two games in the fall of 1967. Betts believed he had as good a chance as any to compete for playing time that spring, but he injured his knee in a pick-up basketball game that winter and missed all of spring practice. When he returned in the fall, he was at the bottom of the depth chart.

That's when his positional sojourning began. He switched to tailback after senior Ron Johnson hurt his thumb in summer camp, but he grew disenchanted after running backs coach Tony Mason didn't put him on the travel roster for a game at Duke. The following week in practice, he was invited to join the wide receivers and finished the season at that position. He played quarterback and defensive back under Schembechler.

The one play Betts clearly remembers from his career is one that went for an Ohio State touchdown in the 1970 game in Columbus. The Wolverines were in man coverage, and he was responsible for tight end Jan White. Judging from what he'd seen on film, Betts expected White to run a delay over the middle, but he stayed in to block. Caught too close to the line of scrimmage, Betts was a step late getting back to stop a touchdown pass from Rex Kern to Bruce Jankowski that propelled the Buckeyes to a 20-9 victory.

Working on his degree in education, Betts injured his left eye in a freak accident while student teaching. He had a 70 percent loss of vision in that eye, which dramatically hurt his depth perception the following summer when he tried out for the New York Jets, who'd drafted him the previous spring. The Jets cut him in training camp, and he failed to stick after a tryout with the Minnesota Vikings. He later played for a short time with the Hamilton Tiger-Cats of the Canadian Football League. He returned to Michigan to complete his degree, and he joined Schembechler's staff as a graduate assistant.

Betts worked for Goodyear for two years before returning to Michigan, this time as an academic advisor for athletes. In 1979, he joined a Boston finance company that eventually transferred him to Chicago. When the company closed that office, he stayed and sold insurance until he returned to the Ann Arbor area to work for Don Coleman, another former Michigan player, who'd opened an advertising agency. He has worked the past 15 years for Domino's Pizza, where he is in charge of minority recruitment.

Betts and his wife, Marty, have been married 19 years. They have two sons: Evan, 15; and, Eric, 13. The family lives in Milan, Michigan.

"In spite of whatever bad things might have happened at Michigan, the good things far exceeded them," Betts said. "Having had the experience of playing under both Bump (Elliott) and Bo was valuable. There was a huge contrast there, but each of them gave us skills we could use. Bump taught us how to be gracious. Bo gave us the discipline to be gracious, but he also taught us to be as tenacious as you had to be. One thing I can say about Michigan, it has truly served me well over the years."

CARLITOS BOSTIC

In hindsight, Carlitos Bostic wishes he'd had a little more insight.

Had he been less stubborn and more willing to listen to his coaches, who he realizes now had his best interests in mind when they asked him to switch positions, he might have had an entirely different college career. He's proud of what he did in five seasons at Michigan, but he believes he could have done so much more.

Bostic was recruited as an outside linebacker, and he refused to budge from that position. Early on, Michigan defensive coaches sensed that he had the size, speed and talent to become an exceptional defensive end. He grudgingly switched positions for a couple of weeks in 1986, but he gave a half-hearted effort and soon was back at linebacker. Friends from his old neighborhood applauded his determination to stick to his guns. He wishes now he hadn't listened to them.

"The move (to defensive end) failed because I refused to wholeheartedly accept the change and try my best, because I knew in my mind that I was an outside linebacker," he said. "Honestly, being an older and more mature man now, I believe that would have been my best option. (Former Michigan star) Ian Gold is a great example of how you make a change. He was asked to go from running back to linebacker, and he did his best at his new position. He might have been an average running

CARLITOS BOSTIC
Michigan letterman: 1985-1987

Position: Linebacker **Number:** 99
Hometown: Ypsilanti, Michigan

Career defense: 27 tackles, 1 sack, 2 forced fumbles
Top game: 3 tackles, 1 forced fumble at Minnesota, 1987

back, but he was a great linebacker. That move paid off for him—very well.

"I had a conversation with (Coach Gary) Moeller when he was an assistant coach with the Detroit Lions, and he told me he believed I would still have been in the NFL if I had stayed as a defensive lineman. That was the biggest compliment I ever had in terms of someone believing in my abilities. I look at guys like Warren Sapp. He's not that big, but he has great hips and feet, and is a thinker. That's the way I played the game. I just chose not to make the change."

Growing up in nearby Ypsilanti, Michigan, Bostic often told friends he would some day play for Michigan. They'd laugh at him, because he wasn't very big at the time. He went on a church field trip to a game at Michigan Stadium when he was nine years old, and he announced to one of the adult chaperones the minute the group walked into the stadium that he would be a Wolverine one day. "I can remember watching Florida State and Notre Dame on television, but to see Michigan in person as a kid, that made such an impression," he said. "That first experience blew me away."

Bostic was one of several Division I prospects to come out of Ypsilanti High School in the early 1980s. As a fullback, he'd blocked for Eric Ball, who went to UCLA. His best friend was defensive back Steve Lawrence, who played at Notre Dame. One of the games he remembers most as a player was Michigan's 24-23 win at Notre Dame in 1986. Bostic, who played defensive end in that game, says he wanted to show Lawrence that he could be a difference-maker for the Wolverines. He still keeps a photograph of himself hugging Lawrence immediately after the game that appeared the following Monday in *The Michigan Daily*.

He delivered one of his biggest plays on special teams at Minnesota in 1987. The Wolverines trailed at halftime, and Coach Bo Schembechler had spent much of the intermission yelling at his players. Because Michigan was set to kick off to start the second half, members of the kickoff team talked among themselves about the need to make some kind of play. Bostic did just that, as he slammed into the Minnesota return man and forced a fumble that his teammates recovered deep in Golden Gophers territory. The touchdown sparked Michigan to a 30-20 victory. "Coaches like to say that one play can make a career," Bostic said. "Just to be part of the team and add to the team's success meant a lot to me."

Bostic signed with the Detroit Lions as a free agent in 1988. Ironically, he hoped to get a chance to play defensive end, but the Lions moved him to inside linebacker and paired him with fellow rookie, Chris

Spielman. Bostic got through training camp, but did not make the final cut. His agent then hooked him up with the Canadian Football League's Toronto Argonauts, for whom he played for two seasons. He then played two seasons of American football in Finland.

He was unsure what to do next after he returned to the United States. He coached for a season at Division III Trinity College in Connecticut before returning to Ypsilanti, where he helped coach the high school team for a season. He then joined the Marine Corps. "I had talked to my uncle about the military, and he thought I would be good as an officer," Bostic said. "He felt the discipline and the psychology of military living and training would do me a lot of good. It did." Bostic graduated from officers' candidate school as a second lieutenant and served for four years in motor transportation at Camp Pendleton in California. He served in "Operation Restore Hope" in Somalia. He retired from the Marines as a captain in 1995.

Bostic now works as a safety officer for Saginaw-based Spence Brothers Construction, which was helping to build the new Bio-Medical Research Building at Michigan. He and his wife, Yolanda, have been married nine years. They have two daughters—Brittany, 13, and Courtney, 6—and are expecting a son, whom they plan to name Carlitos Jr. "C.J. Bostic ... that will be a good linebacker name," he said.

From time to time, Michigan coaches ask Bostic, now 39, to speak to current players who struggle when asked to change positions. He says he explains that he had the opportunity to make a change that could have helped him and the team, but that he blew it. He wants anyone willing to listen to learn from his mistake.

"What I learned from my time here and later as a coach is that when a coach asks you to do something, it's not only for you, it's for the team," he said. "That sounds kind of corny. But if you can perform better, if you can raise your abilities and understand that the coach is doing it for you, you can excel. No coach wants to see his player fail, but I used to think that. The bottom line is, they want you to play better. I try to let kids know that they need to listen to their coaches. I learned that the hard way."

Where Have You Gone?

TONY BRANOFF

A 100-yard rushing performance is considered the norm these days for a good running back, but it was a special accomplishment when Tony Branoff was lugging the ball for Michigan in the 1950s. He had two such games during his career, and each stands out because it was such a rarity.

Branoff ran for 113 yards and a touchdown his sophomore season to help spark Michigan to a 20-0 victory against Ohio State. He says it was the best game of his career. "When we ran to the weak side, it seemed to be open," he said. "We had some good blockers, and I was smart enough to follow them." Two seasons later, he ran for 103 yards and the Wolverines' only touchdown in a 25-6 loss at Illinois. In between, his best game, statistically speaking, was a 62-yard performance against Iowa, also during his senior season.

"That shows you the kind of offense we ran," the 70-year-old Branoff said, noting that Coach Bennie Oosterbaan's single wing did not feature any one running back. "I was looking at my statistics the other day, and there's really no way to compare them to what you see today. I led the team in rushing in 1953 with 501 yards, and I led the team again in 1955 with 387. You wouldn't see that today."

TONY BRANOFF
Michigan letterman: 1952-1955

Position: Halfback **Number:** 17
Hometown: Flint, Michigan
Career rushing: 292 carries, 1,299 yards, 11 TDs
Top game: 17 carries, 113 yards, 1 TD vs. Ohio State, 1953

Branoff is correct. Since Bo Schembechler arrived at Ann Arbor in 1969, the lowest season total for a team-leading Michigan running back was 574 yards, by freshman Jamie Morris in 1984. In 23 of those 35 seasons, Michigan boasted a 1,000-yard rusher.

What's impressive about Branoff's statistics is that he compiled many of those yards while running on injured knees. He tore cartilage in his left knee during his senior season at Flint Central, which limited his participation in the annual Thanksgiving Day game against Flint Northern at Atwood Stadium. He suffered a similar injury to his right knee during Michigan's game against Army in 1954, his junior season, during which he played just two more games. He started every game at right halfback in 1955, but his mobility was limited because his knees were heavily taped. "I was not the fastest player in the world, so I had to rely on being shifty," he said. "But you sort of lose your speed after you have operations and your knees need to be taped."

Branoff believes he was the first football player to receive an injection of cortisone, the use of which was being pioneered at Michigan. But the shots didn't dissolve the loose cartilage in his knee, as doctors had hoped it would, and he had surgery at the conclusion of the 1954 season.

In the early 1950s, many of the best players in Flint were going to Michigan State, which had just joined the Big Ten. Branoff strongly considered MSU because his brother had just graduated from the business school there, but he believed his best opportunity to play quickly was at Michigan. "State had two full backfields at the time," he recalled. "That's how loaded they were."

In an effort to take advantage of the freshman eligibility rule in place at the time, Branoff left Flint Central in the middle of his senior year and enrolled at Michigan in January of 1952. To make the jump, he had to agree to take a mathematics extension course. He took examinations for that class in stages, so that he didn't finish the class and officially graduate from high school until his junior year at Michigan.

At the conclusion of his senior season, Oosterbaan called Branoff into his office. Ohio State coach Woody Hayes was coaching one of the all-star squads in the East-West Shrine Game, and he'd called Oosterbaan to see if Branoff was interested in playing in the game. Branoff played, but he says he was overshadowed by such future NFL stars as Lenny Moore, Howard "Hopalong" Cassady, Sam Huff and Jim Katkavage. "We really had a talented team."

Branoff was selected by the Chicago Cardinals in the 23rd round of the 1956 NFL Draft, but he decided to pass up a professional career because he worried about the condition of his knees. He says that if he had decided to play professionally, he would have gone to the Canadian Football League to play for Toronto, which would have paid him $16,000. That was twice the salary the top NFL running backs were making at the time.

With a degree from Michigan's School of Literature, Science and the Arts, Branoff worked in sales for a variety of companies for nearly 10 years before he returned to Ann Arbor in 1966 to work for Cushing-Malloy book printers. He eventually became personnel manager, and he retired from the company in April, 2003 after 37 years.

Branoff, who resides in Saline, was divorced in 1972 and has never remarried. He has three sons: Anthony Jr. and twins Terry and Timothy.

Like many former football players, Branoff suffered with arthritic knees for years, and the soreness eventually forced him to give up playing one of his favorite games, paddleball. At age 65, he had both knees replaced. "I had them both done at the same time," he said. "The doctor told me at the time that was a wise choice, and he was right. If I had done just one, I might not have done the other one."

J.D. CARLSON

J.D. Carlson is one of the finest kickers ever to play for Michigan, and he's got his name all over the record book to prove it. What's amazing about those numbers is not that Carlson had success, but that he got the opportunity to kick for Michigan at all. Had it not been for a strange series of circumstances during his senior year in high school and a bit of luck on the part of the Wolverines, he would never have made it to Ann Arbor.

"How I got here is as interesting as the things I accomplished once I did," he said.

Though Carlson was an all-state kicker in 1986 for Tallahassee Leon High School, one of Florida's prep football powerhouses, he was not heavily recruited. With the help of his high school coach, who had a weekly television show, Carlson put together a highlight tape and sent it to the 20 Division I schools that most interested him. The list included Michigan. He received only one scholarship offer, rejected it and committed to Yale.

Weeks after signing day, Carlson got a call from Michigan assistant coach Bobby Morrison, who asked if he was still interested in the Wolverines. Morrison had held on to Carlson's tape, and that proved to be fortuitous, because the kicker who'd committed to Michigan that winter decided to go to another school. Carlson told Morrison he

Photo courtesy of Bob Kalmbach, University of Michigan

J.D. CARLSON
Michigan letterman: 1989-1991

Position: Kicker **Number:** 38 **Hometown:** Tallahassee, Florida
All-Big Ten, 1989-91
Career PATs: 137 of 139; .986 conversion rate is best in school history
Career field goals: 39-of-57
Kicked two game-winners: at UCLA in 1989 and at Ohio State in 1990

intended to go to Yale, but the coach offered to fly him to Ann Arbor to attend Michigan's spring game. As it turned out, Carlson had never taken a fifth official visit to a prospective school, so he accepted. "I met Bo (Schembechler) and some of the guys in the incoming (freshman) class, and I got a chance to see Ann Arbor," he said. "I recognized right away that this is a phenomenal place." Carlson told Yale coaches he planned to walk on at Michigan.

Carlson says he was unprepared in many respects for many of his first college experiences. "I'm a pretty laid-back guy, and I tend to take things day to day," he admitted. "I did not have a grand scheme worked out in my mind in terms of my college or football careers. I just knew that I could be part of something special, and I was willing to see where it would take me." He arrived in Ann Arbor with no winter clothes. "I still remember walking to class in the snow," he said, laughing. "I had no socks on, and I was getting snow in my shoes. I kept thinking: 'I have to do something about this.'"

Carlson considered transferring after his freshman season to Yale, where he would immediately challenge for the starting job. Though he was now on scholarship at Michigan, he was discouraged at being relegated to a backup role behind Mike Gillette for one more season. Carlson decided to stay, in part because Schembechler assured him in the spring that he would play a more significant role in the future. By then, he'd discovered a more important reason to remain at Michigan: He admired and had become friends with many of his classmates on the team, such as offensive lineman Greg Skrepenak and defensive back Tripp Welborne. "Those are some of the most outstanding people I have ever met," he said. "It was not something where they looked at me as if I was their best buddy, but I knew that if I hung in there, I'd be part of something special."

Carlson proved to be something special. He never missed an extra point during two of his three seasons as the starter—he was 52 for 52 in 1991 and 47 for 47 in 1990—and no Michigan kicker attempted (139) or made (137) more PATs in his career than he did. He is third on Michigan's career list with 39 field goals and 57 attempts. His .929 conversion rate on field goals in 1989—he hit 13 of his 14 attempts—is a school record. He tied a school record with five field goals in a 22-17 win against Illinois in 1990. He kicked 11 field goals of 40 or more yards and two of more than 50 yards.

Carlson attributes much of his consistency on extra points to the fact that he had the same snapper and holder, Steve Everett and Ken Sollom, pretty much throughout his career. "When you get that kind of consistency, it is a very easy kick," he said. "You're confident the other guys will do their jobs, so there's really no reason to miss." He says he believes he earned the respect of his teammates because he worked as hard on his kicking in practice as they did at their positions. "Knowing all those guys depended on me pushed me to work harder," he said. "At the end of the day, I was the guy selected to make the kick for the team. I went out with confidence because I had done it so much in practice, and the guys had confidence in me."

He twice repaid that confidence in spectacular fashion by kicking game-winning field goals. His 37-yarder with no time remaining gave Michigan a 16-13 win at Ohio State and a share of the Big Ten championship in 1990. A season earlier, he'd kicked a 24-yarder with a second remaining to give the Wolverines a come-from-behind 24-23 win at UCLA.

Carlson treasures the kick at Ohio State more than any other, he says, because it gave him a shot at redemption. Minutes earlier, he'd missed a short field-goal attempt that would have given the Wolverines the lead. But needing a win to clinch the outright Big Ten title and a trip to the Rose Bowl, the Buckeyes elected to run on fourth down deep in their own territory. The Michigan defense held, and Carlson made the most of his second chance.

Carlson said his kicking performance in the UCLA game ensured that he would have a long Michigan career. During a loss to Notre Dame in the season opener the previous weekend, two of his kickoffs had been returned for touchdowns, and he'd missed an extra point and botched an onside kick. But against UCLA, Carlson was perfect on the first four field-goal attempts of his career, and his onside kick late in the game set up his game-winner.

Because of his interest in ecology and the outdoors, Carlson earned bachelor's and master's degrees in biology, and he returned to Michigan to earn an MBA. He has been employed as a certified public accountant in the audit division for the Detroit office of Price Waterhouse Coopers.

He met Paula Waterstradt at a party his roommates threw following the Wolverines' return from the 1992 Rose Bowl, his last game as a Michigan football player. The two were married in 1994, and they live in Plymouth, Michigan.

Carlson said he was able to bounce back from misses, particularly the one at Ohio State in 1990, because he focused on success and did not worry about failure. "That allowed me to stay positive and recover quickly if I missed," he said. "That's what kicking is all about. I will forever be prepared for the rest of my life because I have experienced some of the biggest swings in emotion in a short period of time. Not much fazes me now."

Where Have You Gone?

DANA COIN

Dana Coin might be best remembered by Michigan football fans for his kicking exploits, but Coin never considered himself a specialist as kickers and punters do in today's game. His head coach, Bo Schembechler, didn't consider him a specialist, either, and Coin got that message loud and clear the first time the two met in 1969.

"When Bo first talked to me, all he said was, 'There will be no specialists on this team,'" Coin recalled. "That was the way it was when I played at Michigan. You were a football player first. If you could do something as a specialist, that was a bonus."

Coin was a linebacker first and a kicker second, and he wasn't alone in doing double duty. On the '69 team, he backed up Marty Huff at linebacker and handled kickoffs. Frank Titus played guard and kicked extra points. Tim Killian played center and kicked field goals. Split end Paul Staroba was the punter. "It was so much different than today's football," Coin said. "During practice, you were playing linebacker, not over on some other field kicking balls back and forth. If you were a specialist back then, unless it was a special situational drill, you were on the field early or after practice. That meant you got to travel. There were only 50-man travel squads back then, so you had to be able to do something else."

DANA COIN
Michigan letterman: 1969-1971

Position: Linebacker/kicker **Number:** 36
Hometown: Pontiac, Michigan

Career defense: 54 tackles, 1 fumble recovery
Career field goals: 13 of 27 **Career long:** 42 yards, 1970 vs. Arizona
Top season: 55 of 55 on extra points, 1971

Still, fans could tell Coin was a specialist. Because he used a straight-ahead style, like Lou Groza of the Cleveland Browns, he wore a squared-toe shoe on his right foot the entire game, even when he was playing linebacker.

At the start of his junior season, 1970, Coin handled kickoffs and field-goal attempts. Killian kicked extra points until mid-season, when his inconsistency prompted Schembechler to hand that job to Coin, too. Coin did all three jobs the rest of his career.

Coin had a remarkable career as a kicker, particular during his senior season. He kicked a 42-yard field goal—then the longest in Michigan history—against Arizona in 1970. In a 63-7 win against Iowa that same season, he kicked nine extra points—the second highest total in school history. For the season, he hit all 55 of his extra-point attempts—a perfect mark that set an NCAA record at the time and still stands today as the school record. His 25-yard field goal with 26 seconds remaining in the next-to-last game of the 1971 season at Purdue gave Michigan a 20-17 win and the outright Big Ten championship.

Pressure was never an issue for Coin, and he believes that was because he played another position and didn't have time to fret about having to kick a critical field goal or extra point. "My head was into the game the whole time," he explained. "Mental toughness is so crucial, and that's something that gets developed as you play. (Coordinator) Jim Young taught the entire defense a technique called 'visualization,' which is the concept of seeing yourself as being successful. I attribute my doing so well my senior year to that (concept)."

Coin played linebacker and running back, and he kicked and punted, at Pontiac (Michigan) Northern High School. Northern athletic director Hercules Renda, a former Michigan football player, convinced Coin early on that he had the ability to play at the Division I-A level. But Coin's initial interest in Michigan was because of its academic reputation. His father wanted him to be an engineer, so Michigan coaches made certain Coin toured the university's engineering laboratories on his official visit. Once he saw them, he was hooked.

After graduating from Michigan with a degree in education in 1972, Coin hoped to get a tryout with a National Football League team. He wasn't drafted, but a scout for the Washington Redskins told him the team was interested in signing him as a free agent to kick and play linebacker. Redskins officials contacted Coin's agent, who told them he was attempting to work out a better deal for his client. He didn't, and Coin never got a professional tryout. "I got lost in the shuffle," he said. "If I had to do it again, I would represent myself."

Coin coached and taught in Dowagiac, Michigan, for a year and then returned to the Michigan football program as a graduate assistant. A year later, he headed to nearby Eastern Michigan University as defensive coordinator with Michigan assistant George Mans, who'd been named the Hurons' head coach. Among the players Coin coached in his brief time at EMU were John Banazak and Ron Johnson, both of whom had great careers in the NFL. Mans quit after 2 1/2 years because of a disagreement with EMU's athletic director, and Coin left coaching for good.

Terry Barr, another former Michigan football player, hired Coin as a salesman for his company, Terry Barr Sales, which represented manufacturers to the automotive industry. Coin worked for Barr for nine years and then started a similar business. In 1991, Coin sold his business to a partner and went to work for an automotive electronics manufacturing company, Jabil Circuits, and eventually took charge of its global automotive accounts. He left Jabil in 2003 to go to work for a competitor, Celestica Corp., the manufacturing arm of IBM.

Coin married his first wife, Debbie, during his junior year at Michigan, and he has two children, Deric and Darci, by that marriage. The couple divorced after eight years. He remarried in 1981, to Christine, and the couple had one child, Alyson. Christine died in 1995. He remarried in 1999, to Linda, who has two children, Kayla and Alec, from a previous marriage. The couple has a child of their own, Julia, who was born in 2001. Coin and his family live in Clarkston, Michigan.

Coin said he tries to draw daily in his business from his experiences at Michigan, particularly those involving teamwork. "There's no question I like working in a team environment," he said. "The power of the team makes you successful. Bo taught us that. No one is more important than anyone else. Bo used to say that you either got better every day or you got worse, but you never stayed the same. If you didn't get better, you took a step backward. It's as true today as it was then."

GARVIE CRAW

Members of Bo Schembechler's first Michigan team like to tease former teammate Garvie Craw that no running back in history got more mileage out of fewer carries than he did.

While that's not completely accurate, it's a good indicator of Craw's productivity in 1969, his senior season. If the Wolverines had the ball near the goal line, chances were Craw would get it. He scored a team-high 12 touchdowns that season, averaging one every 10 carries. The team's leading rusher that season, Billy Taylor, averaged a touchdown every 20 carries.

Certainly, it is an enviable mark that few players have surpassed. For instance, Anthony Thomas, the school's all-time leading rusher, averaged a touchdown every 17 carries during his career. One ex-Wolverine who did have a better mark was the legendary Tom Harmon, who scored a touchdown every eight times he carried the ball.

There were good reasons Craw scored as often as he did in 1969. For one thing, he never lost a yard on any of his 117 carries, so he could be counted on to move the pile forward in short-yardage situations. For another, he earned Schembechler's admiration because of his willingness to do anything that was asked of him in the backfield.

GARVIE CRAW
Michigan letterman: 1967-1969

Position: Fullback **Number:** 48
Hometown: Montclair, New Jersey

Career rushing: 227 carries, 752 yards, 13 TDs
Top game: 17 carries, 56 yards, 2 TDs vs. Ohio State, 1969

"With Bo, you blocked, and he would reward the fullback—me—for that because he knew I would get that extra half-yard we'd need," Craw said. "When your tackle is Dan Dierdorf and tight end is Jim Mandich, that's a lot easier to do. Bo gave me the ball a lot in short yardage. He knew I wouldn't hesitate. He knew that if there was a little bit of room, I'd get a first down or a touchdown."

A native of Montclair, N.J., Craw hadn't thought much about Michigan until he attended a dinner in New York City for many of the area's top high school recruits. There, he met Michigan coach Bump Elliott and was immediately impressed by him. He was even more impressed by Penn State athletic director Ernie McMillan, who told the players that if they ever had the opportunity to attend Michigan, they should take advantage of it. Ultimately, Craw had to choose between Michigan and Ohio State, the first school to recruit him. He chose Michigan because of Elliott and Michigan Stadium.

For a short time his sophomore season, Michigan used Craw as a pooch punter. Because he could not straighten one arm out to get full leg extension, the most he could kick the ball was 30 yards. But he got great hang time. Late in the season opener against Duke, Craw sliced the ball off the side of his foot and out of bounds at the 2-yard line. The Wolverines capitalized to get excellent field position on their next series, and were able to kick the deciding field goal in a 10-7 win. The following weekend at California, Craw kicked the ball straight up in the air, and he downed it himself for a three-yard punt. That was the last punt he ever attempted.

He started that season as a halfback, but Michigan coaches liked his blocking so much that they asked him to move to fullback. He agreed because he wanted to play, but also because the position fit his rough-and-tumble personality: He liked to hit people. By his junior season, he was a fixture in Michigan's strong running game.

"The thing about blocking, if you had a running back who could read blocks, he made you look great," Craw said. "Ron Johnson was great at that. In that (1968) game where he had 347 yards against Wisconsin, we ran pretty much between the tackles. The conditions were lousy. Their linebacker would try to dig in, and I would just line my facemask up between his numbers and bury him. I'd look up and see the white fiberglass bottoms of Ronnie's shoes as he went by."

Johnson's prolific game—still the best individual rushing performance in school history—proved to be the highlight of the season. A week later in the season finale at Ohio State, the eventual national champion Buckeyes manhandled and embarrassed the Wolverines, 50-14. It was

Elliott's last game as head coach. He soon was replaced by Schembechler, an intense, no-nonsense disciplinarian who would remold the program in his own personality. "Bo called me in right after he was introduced as head coach," Craw recalled. "First, he said, 'I understand you're a hell of a football player.' Then he said, 'I hear you hang around in bars, and if you continue to do that, you're off the team.' I was 21 at that point, so I was old enough. But he made it very clear to me who was the top dog in that relationship."

Schembechler's first winter training session was tougher than anything Craw had ever experienced or heard about. "I'm not sure (Vince) Lombardi had tougher camps," he said. But Schembechler was determined to get his players into shape, because he wanted to install a new offense that spring and did not want to waste time with conditioning. "We all understood that it was going to be different in terms of discipline and work," he said. "But Bo set the tone. Nobody worked harder than he did. He also understood, coming from Woody Hayes's staff, what the Ohio State game meant."

In many ways, Michigan's stunning 24-12 upset of Ohio State redefined the rivalry. The game certainly established Schembechler's program and re-established Michigan as one of the elite programs in the country. Many observers believe that game is the greatest ever played in the rivalry, but Craw hesitates to agree because he says it would be disrespectful to all of the great players who'd participated in the series. He does, however, believe it is one of the rivalry's 10 best games.

Craw married his wife, Susan, the spring before his senior season. The couple has three children: Stacey, 34; Corey, 33; and, Matt, 24. Craw graduated from Michigan with a degree in English, but he eventually helped found G.X. Clarke and Company, a government securities dealer. One of the other founding partners is Dennis Morgan, who was a linebacker on Michigan's 1967 team.

"The truth is, I've been luckier than smart," Craw said. "I have good guys to work with. And, because I have a degree in English, every single letter that goes out of this place passes my desk."

TOM CURTIS

I f Tom Curtis has any regret about his Michigan football career, it is this: He never got the opportunity to play quarterback, the position he'd played in high school. "Even after I tied the Big Ten record for interceptions as a sophomore, I still wanted to be a quarterback," he said.

But he admits it is a small complaint. When he was coming out of high school in 1966, it was not unusual for college teams to recruit a number of quarterbacks and convert them to other positions. That was because, typically, quarterbacks were the most versatile players on a high school team. Curtis was one of four quarterbacks in his class, and each eventually became a defensive back. In fact, three of them (Curtis, Barry Pierson and Brian Healy) started all 11 games at defensive back in 1969, Bo Schembechler's first season as head coach.

Curtis was a natural at safety. He started three seasons there for the Wolverines and became the greatest pass interceptor in school history. He wore jersey number 25, which, coincidentally, was his number of career interceptions. He intercepted seven passes in Big Ten play in 1967, tying the conference record, and then grabbed 10 in 1968, including nine in conference play. He picked off eight more during his All-America senior season, including two in Michigan's stunning 24-12 upset of defending national champion Ohio State.

TOM CURTIS
Michigan letterman: 1967-1969

Position: Defensive back **Number:** 25
Hometown: Aurora, Ohio

All-American, 1969
Career defense: 123 tackles, 16 pass breakups, 25 interceptions
Top game: 13 tackles, 2 interceptions at Indiana, 1968

"I'm not certain how I did it," he said. "It was a combination of instinct, great hands and quickness—not speed."

Curtis was one of 22 scholarship players from the state of Ohio on the Michigan roster during Schembechler's first season. He had played quarterback at Aurora High School, and he expected to play that position in college. He was heavily recruited by Penn State and Ohio State, but he turned down the latter because he could not imagine ever playing quarterback for the Buckeyes. He had a number of connections to Michigan: One of his high school coaches was a graduate; his father had gotten his Ph.D. from there; and, his grandfather had lived for a time in Ann Arbor. As did most Ohio players who chose Michigan, Curtis got a lot of guff in his hometown for his decision, but, he adds: "I also transformed my very best friends into Michigan fans."

Curtis never returned one of his interceptions for a touchdown. He came close during a 34-7 win against Wisconsin in 1968, when he was hauled down from behind three yards from the end zone. He said he would have scored had he not badly sprained his ankle earlier in the game. Though his ankle was still in bad shape the following weekend, he played against Ohio State in Columbus. "I was in another world out there," he recalled. "I was so shot up (with pain killers) that I have no idea what was going on. That was unfortunate, because that was the only game I ever played in the Horseshoe (Ohio Stadium)." Maybe it's just as well he doesn't remember much about the game, because the Buckeyes hammered the Wolverines that afternoon, 50-14.

Curtis had been a multi-sport athlete in high school, and he'd hoped to play baseball his last two years at Michigan. He'd already gotten permission to do it from Bump Elliott, but Schembechler was not as accommodating. The new coach told Curtis he could play baseball but only if he did not miss one spring practice. With the baseball team headed to Arizona for its spring trip, something had to give. Curtis gave up any notion of playing baseball.

The '69 team began the season 3-2, with losses to Missouri and Michigan State. Curtis, who had only three interceptions through six games, says he played the worst game of his career in the 23-12 loss to the Spartans. On the bus ride home from East Lansing, he decided he had to improve his play. A week later at Minnesota, though he did not intercept a pass, he played one of his finest games and was subsequently named defensive player of the game. "Those two games were a wake-up call for me," he said. "In my mind, I felt I was deteriorating (as a player). I was determined to finish the season strong."

Like every Michigan veteran, Curtis had anticipated the rematch with top-ranked Ohio State in Ann Arbor. Because of the Big Ten's no-repeat rule, which prevented the Buckeyes from making a second consecutive trip to the Rose Bowl, the Wolverines knew they were headed to the bowl after they'd won at Iowa the previous weekend. But the Wolverines wanted to go to Pasadena as Big Ten champions, not as runners-up. Michigan players were so focused on the game that they were oblivious to any of the hype surrounding it. Curtis was stunned when friends in Aurora told him Ohio State was favored by a whopping 17 points. The Wolverines didn't think of themselves as underdogs, he says. They expected to win the game, because they believed they owed the Buckeyes.

The defense played a key role in the upset, as it shut down the vaunted Ohio State offense. Curtis grabbed two of Michigan's five interceptions, but the play he remembers most from the game is stuffing fullback Jim Otis one on one at the line of scrimmage.

"I don't think we recognized it at the time for what it was," Curtis said when asked about the significance of the victory. "It has gone down as one of the greatest upsets in college football history, but we don't think of it that way. For us, it was confined to Michigan-Ohio State, and we were happy and very proud to have redeemed what had happened the year before. People would ask me what it was like to play in front of the (then) largest crowd in history, and I never paid a bit of attention. I was concentrating so much on what was going on in the game, it was like being in a vacuum. I could have been playing in front of 200 people in Aurora. That meant nothing."

The Baltimore Colts drafted Curtis the following spring, and, as a rookie, he helped them beat Dallas in the Super Bowl. After a second season with the Colts, he was traded to the Los Angeles Rams, who quickly cut him. Miami coach Don Shula immediately picked him up, but Curtis injured his knee in a preseason game and missed the Dolphins' perfect Super Bowl season. He tried to come back the following season, but could not. His football career was over.

Curtis earned a degree in economics from Michigan, but he has worked as a sports journalist since leaving pro football. He owns *Dolphins Digest*, a weekly tabloid-style newspaper that covers the Miami team. He also helps to publish similar weekly newspapers that cover the Pittsburgh Steelers and the Philadelphia Eagles.

He lives in Miami with Debbie, his wife of 30 years. The two met at Michigan. His daughter, Tammi, also is a Michigan graduate. She is married to Jason Carr, the son of Michigan head coach Lloyd Carr. Curtis's sons, Brad and Matthew, both live and work in the Miami area.

Curtis actually did play one game at quarterback for Michigan: for the freshman team against Wisconsin in 1966. He threw one touchdown pass in that game, and former teammates still remember it. "At a reunion last year (for the 100th Michigan-Ohio State game, Billy Harris announced to everyone that he was the only guy to ever catch a touchdown pass from Tom Curtis," he said.

Where Have You Gone?

BILL DALEY

Bill Daley never planned to attend Michigan, much less play for the Wolverines. He was Minnesota born and bred, and he'd already played three seasons in the early 1940s for the University of Minnesota. But because of the national upheaval caused by World War II, Daley played one season for Michigan. It was a season he says he will never forget.

"I was a lucky guy," Daley said. "I got to play for two great schools, but playing at Michigan was one of the greatest thrills I could have had. When I was at Michigan, I was the happiest guy in the world. I always thought being in Ann Arbor was ideal. It had something Minneapolis, being a big city, never did. It was a wonderful situation."

And that's saying something, considering the Minnesota teams on which he played won national championships in 1940 and 1941 and narrowly missed winning another one in 1942. The games with Michigan those three seasons were all close, but the Golden Gophers won them all.

Michigan's 7-6 loss in Minneapolis in 1940 was maybe the greatest disappointment in the storied career of Michigan's first Heisman Trophy winner, Tom Harmon, because it cost the Wolverines the chance to win the Big Nine and national titles. Harmon never scored a point in three

BILL DALEY
Michigan letterman: 1943

Position: Fullback **Number:** 45
Hometown: St. Cloud, Minnesota

All-American, 1943
Career rushing: 120 carries, 817 yards, 9 TDs
Top game: 26 carries, 216 yards, 2 TDs vs. Northwestern, 1943

games against Minnesota, and he missed a critical extra point in the '40 loss. The Wolverines finished 7-1 overall that season and were ranked third nationally behind Minnesota and Stanford.

"Harmon was a big man, and he did everything for them," Daley recalled when asked about the game his freshman season. "But he missed a kick that time, and I think he missed one the year before, too. But he wasn't the only star. Michigan had (halfback) Forrest Evashevski and a really good fullback (Bob Westfall). That combination was very potent. We were lucky to beat them that season."

A native of Melrose, Minnesota, Daley almost certainly would have played a fourth season for the Golden Gophers if the United States had not entered the war. Daley enlisted in the navy and, because of his college background, was selected to attend a midshipman academy at Columbia University in New York City. He was ordered to report to Michigan because it had a Naval reserve officer training program, and he stayed in Ann Arbor for six months until there was an opening in the program at Columbia.

Recruits were expected to remain in good physical shape, so Daley was given a choice: He could participate in navy physical education classes; or, he could work out with the Michigan football team. Remembering Daley's prowess from his Minnesota playing days, Michigan head coach Fritz Crisler begged him constantly to work out with the Wolverines. Daley finally agreed, and once he got a football back into his hands, he was hooked.

A 6-2, 210-pound fullback, Daley had been one of Minnesota's biggest players, which was important in the Golden Gophers' powerful single-wing attack. Daley simply took the snap from center and plowed into the line. The single wing Michigan used was more intricate and relied more on deception, and Daley found it difficult to adapt to the spinning moves required of the fullback. Running backs coach Earl Martineau finally told Daley to forget about spinning and to run straight ahead as he had always done.

Daley was a great addition to the Michigan backfield. He led the Wolverines in rushing in 1943, gaining 817 yards in 120 carries. His 6.8-yard average per carry was the same as Harmon's in 1939, and no leading Michigan rusher since has equaled that mark. He finished seventh in the Heisman Trophy voting that season.

Daley delivered his best performance—an amazing 250 yards—during a 21-7 win against a Northwestern team that featured Otto Graham. Daley also played well against his former team, Minnesota, helping the Wolverines to post a 49-6 triumph that snapped a nine-game losing streak to the Golden Gophers. "I had to go to Chicago to see a doctor there about my leg, so I rode on the train that far with the Minnesota team," he recalled. "They were pretty downcast (about the loss)."

After graduating from midshipman school in 1944, Daley was shipped to Florida for amphibious training. He was en route to the Pacific when the war ended in August, 1945, but he remained overseas for a time. While in Shanghai, China, he participated in an Army-Navy football game.

Daley had been approached during his training period in Florida about playing in a new professional football league, the All-American Football Conference, that organizers planned to start after the war. He eventually signed a contract worth $30,000—a enormous amount at that time—and wound up playing four seasons for three teams: the Brooklyn Dodgers, the Chicago Rockets, and the New York Yankees.

His professional career finished, Daley returned to Minneapolis to complete his degree at Minnesota. He then went to work for a local radio station, and his duties included helping to broadcast Minnesota football games. Daley was able to watch halftime performances for the first time, and he says he was most impressed any time he got the chance to watch the Michigan marching band perform.

The 84-year-old Daley and his wife, Melba, celebrated their 32nd anniversary this year. They live in Edina, a suburb of Minneapolis. The couple owns an art gallery inside the Hyatt Regency Hotel in downtown Minneapolis. The gallery specializes in pin-up prints, including some that pre-date World War II, and it has a large collection of original illustrations by Norman Rockwell and Gil Elvgren.

Daley's one disappointment about his college football career is that he never played on a team that beat Notre Dame. His Minnesota teams had always lost to the Fighting Irish, and he hoped things would be different at Michigan. They weren't. Notre Dame defeated Michigan, 35-12, in 1943. It was the only loss the Wolverines suffered that season. "I wanted to beat them so bad, and I played one of the best games of my life," he said. "But it wasn't to be."

GENE DERRICOTTE

As he took stock of the many talented players enrolling in school, Gene Derricotte wasn't certain whether he had a football future when he returned to Michigan after his service in the Army Air Corps during World War II. Would there be a place for him in the Wolverines' lineup? Adding to his concern was the fact that he'd been accepted into the School of Pharmacy, and the dean told him that none of his students had ever played football because of the heavy academic demands.

But Derricotte was every bit as determined as he was talented. He told the dean that he would attend classes year-round—he planned to complete as many laboratory requirements as possible in the summer— to make time for football in the fall, and the dean agreed to create a schedule that would work. And, because Coach Fritz Crisler insisted that each player get a degree, Derricotte could arrive late to practice if there was a time conflict with an afternoon class. "Fritz cared little about pro football," Derricotte said. "He wanted us to get on with our careers, so he wanted us to finish school. It was a different time altogether."

It was certainly a memorable time for Michigan football. The Wolverines won Big Ten championships in 1947 and 1948, crushed Southern Cal in the 1948 Rose Bowl, shared the national championship with Notre Dame following the '47 season and won it outright in '48.

GENE DERRICOTTE
Michigan letterman: 1944, 1946-1948

Position: Halfback **Number:** 41
Hometown: Defiance, Ohio

Career rushing: 171 carries, 857 yards, 11 TDs
Career punt returns: 13.8 yards per return

Derricotte was a key to the program's success. He started at strong safety on a ferocious defense that gave up an average of five points a game during a 23-game winning streak from 1946 through 1948. He played some at halfback in Michigan's prolific single-wing attack. He also was dangerous on punt returns, averaging 13.9 yards in 1946 and 24.8 yards in 1947.

"You could see as guys returned from the military in 1946 that we were going to have a great team," he said. "We were four and five guys deep at every position. Crisler had already started free substitutions. What we were able to do is that everybody could play, and we were great because of that."

Derricotte, now 78, grew up in the northwest corner of Ohio, in the small town of Defiance, where he was the star of the high school football team in 1943. He visited Ohio State that fall, but, because most men his age were being drafted, the school's freshman coach told him to come out for football only after he'd completed his military service. Because Derricotte was only 17 when he graduated from high school, Michigan coaches invited him to enroll in school until he was ordered to report for duty. "That was a great invitation," he said. "I was leaning toward Michigan anyway."

Derricotte started nine of the Wolverines' 10 games in 1944, and he led the team in total offense (618 yards) and punt returns (averaging 6.3 yards a return). He was drafted into the Army immediately after the season and was ordered to report to artillery school in North Carolina, but because he had taken some college classes, he was quickly transferred to the Army Air Corps and began pilot training in Tuskegee, Alabama. He ultimately learned to fly B-25 bombers, and graduated in the spring of 1946 as a second lieutenant. With the war over, however, Derricotte served only two months before being placed on inactive duty. He returned to Michigan.

The 1946 season would set the tone for the two championship campaigns to follow. The Wolverines opened with two wins, but lost 20-13 to Army, tied Northwestern and then lost a close game to Illinois. They finished the season on a four-game winning streak, and Michigan would not lose again until the 1949 season. Derricotte says he remembers the '46 Army game most, because the Michigan defense had to face a Cadet offense that still featured star running backs Glenn Davis and Doc Blanchard. The loss was a heartbreaking one, he says, because a teammate dropped a pass in the end zone in the game's closing seconds.

Derricotte spent much more time on defense than he did on offense during the '47 season, but he still scored some points. He had a 70-yard touchdown run during a 40-6 win at Wisconsin, and he scored a touch-down on a misdirection play during the 49-0 win against Southern Cal in the Rose Bowl. He remembers the Wisconsin game for another reason, too: Conditions were cold and wet, and on one run around end, he was knocked skidding out of bounds into a puddle of muddy, icy water.

Following the '48 season, Derricotte played briefly for the Cleveland Browns before a knee injury ended his career. He completed his degree in pharmacy in 1950 and worked in that profession until 1954, when he entered Michigan's School of Dentistry. He graduated in 1958 and went into private practice in Detroit until he entered the United States Air Force as a captain in 1962.

After three years at a base in South Dakota, Derricotte was assigned as senior dental officer for the Second Air Division at Tan Son Nhut air base in South Vietnam. He returned to the United States after a 13-month tour and was promoted to major. He completed six more assignments, including one at the Air Force Academy in Colorado Springs, before retiring as a colonel in 1985. He worked until his retirement in 2002 as an assistant professor in the Department of Oral and Maxillofacial Surgery at the University of Texas Dental School in San Antonio.

Derricotte and his wife, Jeanne, have been married since 1955. A graduate of the Academy of Arts and Crafts in Detroit, she works as a multi-media artist and graphics designer. The couple has one son, Robert, a graduate of Southern Illinois University who now works for a Georgia pharmaceutical company.

Father and son attended the 100th Michigan-Ohio State game in Ann Arbor in 2003, and the game rekindled many fond memories. "I have never regretted my decision to attend Michigan, but I remember wondering at the time if I was making the right choice," Dericotte said. "I was a big star in high school, but that was at a small school. You never know how going to a big university will turn out. I just went there determined to do the best I could."

Where Have You Gone?

JIM DETWILER

Jim Detwiler experienced an epiphany the week after Michigan's 17-10 win against Michigan State in 1964. He loved to play football, but the pressure he felt before each game chewed up his insides. He threw up because of nervousness. Worse, every mistake he made during games was a burden that became increasingly difficult to bear.

It all came to a head in that nationally televised game at Spartan Stadium. The Wolverines were dominating, but the game was close. Michigan coaches called for a bootleg pass play, and quarterback Bob Timberlake faked the run so well that the entire MSU defense followed him. That left Detwiler, then a sophomore, uncovered to the opposite side of the field. Timberlake threw him a perfect pass that should have gone for a touchdown, but Detwiler bobbled the ball and stepped out of bounds before gaining control of it. The Wolverines failed to score on the drive.

"The play was so traumatic for me that I became a basket case," Detwiler recalled. "The pressure got to me. The coaches took me out of the game, as much for my good as the good of the team. They were worried—and I was worried—that something like that would happen again. Fortunately we won, so that took me off the hook."

Photo provided by Bentley Historical Library

JIM DETWILER
Michigan letterman: 1964-1966

Position: Halfback **Number:** 48
Hometown: Toledo, Ohio

All-Big Ten, 1966
Career rushing: 179 carries, 788 yards, 7 TDs
Top game: 20 carries, 140 yards, 1 TD at Ohio State, 1966

Detwiler was intensely introspective for much of the following week. He knew he could not continue to put so much pressure on himself so he decided he had to change. "What I realized—and this was more of a religious thing than anything else—was that I had this tendency to put myself in the center of the universe, and I wasn't," he said. "That was probably the turning point of my life. After that, the pressure never happened again. I never puked again before a game, unless I was sick."

His new resolve was tested the very next week. After busting through the line, Detwiler had the football securely tucked under his arm and appeared headed for a touchdown when a Purdue defender hit him squarely from behind and sent the ball sailing into the end zone, where the Boilermakers recovered. The Wolverines went on to suffer their only loss of the season, 21-20. That mistake was not the only costly one Michigan made that afternoon, but a week earlier it would have been a crushing blow to Detwiler's psyche. Not this time. "It didn't bother me like the (mistake) at Michigan State did," he said. "I had rearranged my priorities from the week before. It still hurt, but I knew I had done my best."

Heavily recruited as a prep star in Toledo, Detwiler strongly considered the military academies as a college option. He refused an invitation to visit Ohio State, prompting Coach Woody Hayes to harangue him on the telephone one night for more than half an hour about being disloyal to the state of Ohio. Detwiler chose Michigan because of its football tradition and proximity to home, but he also appreciated Coach Bump Elliott's honesty when it came to recruiting.

Detwiler began his sophomore season as Michigan's third-string left halfback, but he moved into the starting lineup following injuries to John Rowser and Jack Clancy. Both would eventually move to other positions—Rowser to defensive back and Clancy to wide receiver—and go on to play in the National Football League. Ironically, Detwiler's first two games were against Air Force and Navy, two schools that had recruited him. He gained 72 yards against Air Force and 77 against Navy. Those were his two best games that season. "The statistics were pretty spread out that season, but no one was concerned about it," he recalled. "We had the right chemistry, and that was the strength of the team. The coaches felt that any one of the four backs could do well. A lot would depend on what was a good match-up for us."

After the '64 Big Ten championship season, much again was expected of the Wolverines the following season. But Detwiler injured his knee during an August practice and played only three games that season –

enough to cost him a season of eligibility. He had surgery after the Michigan State game to repair a torn anterior cruciate ligament and torn cartilage. He returned to play his senior season, but he never fully recovered from the injury. His knee would swell after every game.

He did save his best game for last, however. The week before the 1966 season finale at Ohio State, the Wolverines scrapped their Wing-T formation in favor of a Power-I, and the Buckeyes never fully adjusted to it. Suddenly the focus of the running game, Detwiler carried 20 times for 140 yards – both career highs. He did it all in the first half, and he was so tired that he did not play a down in the second half. Michigan won, 17-3. "We knew after the first two series that we were the better team," he said. "They couldn't stop us, and they couldn't do much against us. But I'll tell you what: That game got me a pro contract."

Baltimore had two first-round choices in the NFL Draft the following spring. The Colts selected Michigan State defensive lineman Bubba Smith with their first pick and Detwiler with the second one, even though he had told the Colts repeatedly that his knee did not feel right. He went to training camp and was able to play in a couple of preseason games, but he needed surgery and missed the regular season. He tried to make the team the following season, but the knee was never right. His football career was over.

Detwiler did have one memorable moment with the Colts. During one preseason game, he tried to get open on a hook pattern in the middle of the field, but the pass was incomplete. Legendary Colts quarterback Johnny Unitas scolded Detwiler when he returned to the huddle. "He told me my job was not to get open, it was to take the middle linebacker away from the pass," he said. "He knew what was going on. Nobody had ever explained that to me."

One of Detwiler's Baltimore teammates, backup quarterback Gary Cuozzo, was enrolled in the dental program at the University of Tennessee. He explained to Detwiler that he was able to attend classes on a rotating six-month basis so he could also play professional football. Detwiler enrolled in the same program, and he began his dental education while he was trying to rehabilitate his injured knee. Though he never played a down in a regular-season game, the Colts still paid Detwiler his signing bonus, and he used it to pay his dental school tuition.

He graduated from dental school in 1971 and decided to return to the Toledo area. After working one year for a local dentist, he opened his own practice in nearby Perrysburg. Now 59, he plans to continue his practice for another five years or so before turning it over to his younger associate.

Detwiler and his wife, Kathleen, a graduate of Michigan's nursing school, have been married for 36 years. The couple has three children: a son, Mike; and two daughters, Jennifer and Katie.

"I have no regrets about anything I have ever done, so I would not do anything differently," Detwiler said. "There were things I didn't like about football, but it provided a vehicle for me to go to college. I would never have been able to afford to go to dental school without it. I would have a totally different life if I had not played football."

Where Have You Gone?

DAN DWORSKY

Dan Dworsky's college football career is one to which Wally Pipp could relate. Pipp, a first baseman for the New York Yankees in the 1920s, sat out a game with a headache and lost his job to future Hall of Famer Lou Gehrig. Dworsky lost the position he'd hoped to play because he got sick, but a teammate's injury later gave him the opportunity to start at another spot.

A Minneapolis native who played his high school football in Sioux Falls, S.D., Dworsky planned to be a fullback his entire college career. That was the reason he chose Michigan over boyhood favorite Minnesota in 1945: He knew the Wolverines needed a fullback for their single wing. He started his freshman season at fullback, but when he was sidelined for three weeks by the flu he slipped to second on the depth chart. In stepped Jack Weisenberger, who, as it turned out, was better suited for the unique demands of the position in Michigan's offense.

Similarities between Dworsky and Pipp end there, however, because Dworsky didn't drop out of the starting lineup. In fact, he started at fullback late in the '45 season after Weisenberger was injured, and he was the leading rusher in a 7-3 win against Ohio State. But, while Dworsky's days as a fullback were numbered—he played just two seasons at that position before switching to center—he plugged in elsewhere as a starter.

DAN DWORSKY
Michigan letterman: 1945-48

Position: Linebacker/fullback **Number:** 39/59
Hometown: Sioux Falls, South Dakota

Career rushing: 95 carries, 389 yards, 5 TDs

Elsewhere turned out to be at linebacker, and, ironically, he would take advantage of another player's injury to move into that spot. After team captain Joe Ponsetto suffered a season-ending knee injury during a late October win at Illinois in 1945, coaches put Dworsky at linebacker during a scrimmage in practice. Still unhappy that he'd lost the starting fullback job, Dworsky took his frustration out on teammates. He nearly knocked halfback Wally Teninga senseless on one play, prompting head coach Fritz Crisler to shout: "Get Dworsky out of there before he kills someone!"

But Dworsky's thundering tackle had made an impression, and a week later assistant coach Bennie Oosterbaan told him he'd start against Navy at linebacker. He would play the rest of his football career, including one season as a pro, at that position. "I was not typical of the fullbacks at Michigan, because I was not as agile as some of the smaller guys," he said. "I had been a linebacker in high school, so it wasn't strange for me to make that switch. Basically I became a specialist at linebacker. Fritz Crisler initiated the two-platoon system because we had so many outstanding players. We had captains sitting on the bench. When you have that many good players, it made sense to play the best on defense and the best on offense."

The two-platoon system worked well for Michigan, which won Big Ten and national championships in Dworsky's final two seasons, 1947 and 1948. The '47 team gets more publicity because it played in the Rose Bowl and crushed Southern Cal, 49-0. The '48 team could not play in the Rose Bowl because of the Big Nine's no-repeat rule. "Each of those teams had distinct qualities," he recalled. "The '47 team was an evolution from the year before, so we started with the confidence that we had a tremendous team. Going to the Rose Bowl made that year particularly special. With a lot of stars gone and Crisler retired, we didn't know for sure what we had in '48. Our defense was composed of many of the same guys from the year before, and it took our offense a couple of games to realize we were just as good as the year before. I am every bit as proud of that team as the one from the year before."

He played what he considers to be his best game in the '48 Rose Bowl. Dworsky called the defensive signals, and he and his teammates were prepared so thoroughly by Crisler and the coaching staff that they felt they knew as much about the USC offense as the Trojans did. "We were prepared to call the right defense, no matter where (USC) was on the field," he said. "It was a joy to call signals under those circumstances. Crisler said later that I had called a perfect game, but I called what I was taught."

Following his senior season, Dworsky was drafted by the Los Angeles Dons of the All-American Football Conference and the NFL's Green Bay Packers. He opted to play for the Dons, in part because they'd selected him in the first round of the draft and in part because, after his Rose Bowl experience, he wanted to live in southern California. The Dons folded after one season, and Dworsky, who'd struggled with asthma throughout his playing career, decided he'd had enough of football.

He returned to Michigan to complete his degree in architecture, then went back to southern California—this time to stay. After working briefly for several area architectural firms, he opened his own office in 1953. He sold his firm in 2001, though he is still associated with it. He and his wife, Sylvia, an Ohio State graduate, have been married 46 years. They have three children: Douglas, who also is an architect; Laurie; and, Nancy.

Dworsky designed many buildings in the Southwest, including the international terminal at Los Angeles International Airport and the federal courthouse in Las Vegas, but he says the crown jewel of his career is Michigan's Crisler Arena.

During a reunion of the '48 team in Ann Arbor in 1963, Crisler, who was still Michigan's athletic director, asked Dworsky to submit a design for the new basketball arena the university was planning to build next to Michigan Stadium. Dworsky had never designed a sports arena before, but he took on the challenge. He researched arenas around the country, paying particular attention to two in Los Angeles, including UCLA's Pauley Pavilion, which was set to open that year. Dworsky was thoroughly prepared with a design when he met with university officials, and, with Crisler's backing, he got the contract.

"I spent two years on that project, and it was an exciting process from beginning to end," he said. "It still amazes me that I was able to do something like that at my alma mater. And it's funny, because though I spent almost my entire career on the west coast, the building I am best known for is the one I did back east."

BRUCE ELLIOTT

Bruce Elliott started in two Rose Bowls during his Michigan career. He was a sophomore on the 1969 Michigan team that stunned top-ranked and defending national champion Ohio State in what many believe is the most significant game in program history. He was a senior on the only Bo Schembechler-coached team to finish unbeaten and untied in a regular season. He never will forget any of those experiences, he says, but the moment in his career that most stands out is a very personal one.

First, a bit of family history is necessary. Elliott's father, Pete, was a mainstay on Michigan's Big Ten and national championship teams of 1947 and 1948, and his uncle, Bump, had starred on the '47 team. Both were All-Americans. The brothers later became rival Big Ten head coaches, Bump at Michigan and Pete at Illinois. Bruce Elliott spent a lot of time as a youngster running around the field at Illinois' Memorial Stadium. He always considered it a special place, even after he decided to attend his father's and his uncle's alma mater.

Pete Elliott was no longer on the Illinois staff by the late 1960s, but many Fighting Illini fans still respected the former head coach and remembered the son from his high school playing days in Champaign, Illinois. The younger Elliott was a backup defensive back on the

BRUCE ELLIOTT
Michigan letterman: 1969-1971

Position: Defensive back **Number:** 21
Hometown: Champaign, Illinois

Career defense: 45 tackles, 7 pass breakups, 5 interceptions
Long return: 40 yards at Illinois, 1969

Michigan team that visited Memorial Stadium in 1969. The Wolverines won 57-0 that afternoon, giving Schembechler the chance to play everyone on the travel squad. Late in the fourth quarter, Elliott intercepted a pass and returned it 40 yards for a touchdown.

"All my teammates came out to congratulate me, but what was unique about it was that the Illinois fans got up and cheered because they saw it was me," Elliott recalled. "It was a great day for me personally. Someone gave me the ball, and I still have it. It wasn't like that was a game-winning play, but it will always be a highlight for me."

Elliott was always a Michigan fan at heart. He got to know Ann Arbor well on visits with his uncle's family, and he sensed early on as he began to consider college choices that he would wind up there, with or without a scholarship. Still, he wanted to play football, so he visited Purdue, Illinois and Duke, and he also considered Miami of Ohio (then coached by a guy named Schembechler). Once his uncle offered him a scholarship to Michigan, however, his choice became an easy one.

Elliott never played for his uncle, however. As a freshman in 1968, he was ineligible to play on the varsity. He accompanied his aunt and cousins to the Ohio State game in Columbus that season, and he watched from the Ohio Stadium stands as the Buckeyes hammered the Wolverines, 50-14. "I was on the demonstration team that week along with guys like Jim Brandstatter and Reggie McKenzie," he recalled. "We tried to simulate that Ohio State team the best we could. I was (quarterback) Rex Kern. That was a tough game to watch. Michigan had a very fine team that year, but Ohio State was a great team."

The game was Bump Elliott's last as head coach. The following winter, Schembechler was hired to replace him. "When Bo got to Michigan, he had a fair amount of talent to deal with," Elliott said. "Bump and his staff had done a good job of recruiting good athletes and quality guys. To Bo's credit, he did a tremendous job of taking everybody and creating a program that I'm not sure anyone has equaled over this period of time. It's just incredible what Bo and (Gary) Moeller and Lloyd (Carr) have done. I think people take that success for granted."

Elliott had been a quarterback in high school, but, as did many of his teammates who were former quarterbacks, he'd moved to the defensive backfield by the time he was a sophomore. He initially played as an extra defensive back on passing downs. Elliott made his first start in the 1970 Rose Bowl against Southern Cal at short-side cornerback after senior Barry Pierson was hurt during practice, and he says he was anxious because he didn't want to make any mistakes. He eventually played every position in the defensive backfield except strong safety. He started at wide-side cornerback his junior and senior seasons.

The 1971 team finished its regular season with an 11-0 record—the only Schembechler-coached team to do that—but the Wolverines lost 13-12 to Stanford in the Rose Bowl on a last-second field goal. The loss remains a difficult one for Elliott and his classmates to accept. "Somebody got hold of a video of the game, and we all got a copy of it at one of our reunions," he said. "I can't remember why, but one day I broke it out to watch it. I just couldn't believe we lost that game. It was very frustrating to watch. It was not for lack of effort. It was not anyone's fault. It was just not to be."

Elliott's goal in college had been to become a college football coach. He enrolled in law school at Miami of Florida, where his father had become athletic director. Elliott was a graduate assistant on the football team while he attended law school. Fresh out of law school, he became a graduate assistant coach on Bill Battle's staff at the University of Tennessee. "Eventually, I realized that the coaching business was pretty tough and that it was easier to get a decent job in the field of law than to get a comparable job in the coaching world," he said. (Former Michigan assistant) Larry Smith offered Elliott a job as an assistant coach on his staff at Tulane, but he decided to try the law business.

He practiced with a large firm in Miami for 2 1/2 years before he and his wife, Cheryl, whom he'd met while both were students at Michigan, decided to move back to southeast Michigan. He joined the Ann Arbor firm of Conlin, McKenney & Philbrick PC in 1978, and he has been a partner since 1985. He and Cheryl have two daughters, Jennifer, a senior at Princeton, and Courtney, a freshman at Duke. Both girls play field hockey. He jokingly laments that he could not convince either of them to play at Michigan.

Elliott's pride in his alma mater is easy to see. Instead of a wedding band, he wears the "M" ring he received at the conclusion of his senior season. "I think I'd die before I ever parted with that ring," he said. "The thing that is great about the Michigan program is that it is something you can always be proud of. The tradition has been carried on since the time of (Fielding) Yost. Bo recognized that from the moment he stepped on the campus. If there is anything to take away from that experience, it's that I had a chance to be a part of that tradition."

Where Have You Gone?

CHRIS FLOYD

Chris Floyd was at a crossroads. He'd been determined to become the featured runner in the Michigan offense as he'd been in high school and, eventually, come to be regarded as one of the great running backs in program history. Trouble was, when he arrived as a freshman in 1994, the Wolverines had a glut of fine tailbacks and a growing shortage of full-backs. When he was asked to back up Che' Foster at fullback for the Holiday Bowl that season, he could see the handwriting on the wall in terms of his college future. What he wanted and what the team needed were two different things.

Now jump ahead to December, 1996. The Wolverines, who'd just upset No. 2 Ohio State in Columbus, were preparing for the Outback Bowl, but Floyd no longer had much joy for the game. Michigan coaches had handed him the starting fullback position because no one else wanted it, he says, but he didn't want it either. His junior season had not gone well, and he seriously considered transferring to another school. Two conversations then changed his mind.

The first actually was a series of heart-to-heart talks with Mike Gittleson, Michigan's strength and conditioning coach, who explained that many fullbacks in school history had had great senior seasons and gone on to play in the National Football League. Gittleson also remind-

CHRIS FLOYD
Michigan letterman: 1994-1997

Position: Fullback **Number:** 7
Hometown: Detroit, Michigan

Career rushing: 148 carries, 623 yards, 2 TDs **Top game:** 7 carries,
41 yards, 1 TD and 4 catches, 35 yards vs. Notre Dame, 1997

ed Floyd each time they talked that Michigan's offense would be more potent if both he and classmate Chris Howard were on the field at the same time. "I pretty much committed (to fullback) then," he said.

Then, just before the Outback Bowl game against Alabama, assistant coach Mike DeBord sought Floyd out while the team was in Tampa. DeBord was set to take over as offensive coordinator the following season, and he promised to utilize the fullback position in the offense more if Floyd would return for his senior season. "I decided to stay and fight the fullback thing out," Floyd said. "True to his word, the following season, he found ways to get me the football."

Head coach Lloyd Carr would later say that Floyd's willingness to commit to the fullback position—as well as his desire to play on special teams—helped to set the tone for the 1997 national championship season. Carr's thinking was this: If Floyd, one of the team's senior leaders, was willing to give up a personal dream for the team's sake, what other player could refuse to do anything that was asked of him?

Floyd had played fullback in Detroit Cooley High School's Wing-T because of his size, but he was the centerpiece of the offense, often carrying the ball as many as 30 times a game. He committed to Colorado on his first recruiting visit, but his mother pressed him to stay close to home. Her wishes finally won out. Floyd played at Michigan as a true freshman, but it was hard for him to distinguish himself against the likes of Tyrone Wheatley, Ed Davis and Tshimanga Biakabutuka. The Wolverines also appeared to be set at fullback, with Foster and Jon Ritchie, but when Ritchie transferred at the end of the regular season, Floyd became a fullback, whether he liked it or not.

While his transition was far from smooth, Floyd had one thing working in his favor: Even at tailback, he loved to block. During a scrimmage early in summer drills his freshman season when he was asked to step in for the injured Wheatley, Floyd saw linebacker Jarrett Irons coming on a blitz and flattened him. As he returned to the huddle, he noticed a smile on running backs coach Fred Jackson's face. "From that point on, it was a love affair for me," Floyd said of blocking. "I loved to beat up on linebackers. As a tailback, I would have done the same thing."

His reputation as a devastating blocker grew with each game in the Wolverines' 1997 championship season. Time after time, he saved quarterback Brian Griese's backside from oncoming pass rushers. If a lineman missed a block, Floyd was there to pick up the defender. He saw each game as a battle of wills between himself and any defender who tried to make a tackle or dared to come into the Michigan backfield. "I knew that eventually, somebody had to give up, either me or the linebacker," he said. "It is so obvious watching film if a guy has thrown in the towel. I refused to have a coach call me out in a meeting and say I gave up. As a Michigan player, you're not going to give up."

Floyd says he played his best game in the '97 season finale against Ohio State. Though the Buckeyes blitzed often, they could not get to Griese because Floyd was there to stop them. "It got to the point where I knew they were coming and they knew I was going to block them," he said. "I would point at the guy blitzing and tell him to bring it on. When you do something like that, it takes the wind out of them. I was not only blocking one guy, sometimes I'd get two at one time." With the game scoreless in the second quarter, Ohio State defensive end Na'il Diggs had what appeared to be a clear shot at sacking Griese. Floyd saw Diggs out of the corner of his eye, turned and knocked him down a second before Griese fired a 37-yard strike to Charles Woodson. That completion set up Michigan's first touchdown in a 20-14 win that clinched the Big Ten title and a trip to the Rose Bowl.

New England selected Floyd in the third round of the 1998 NFL Draft, and he played three seasons for the Patriots. He later played briefly for the Browns, and has had a tryout in the Arena Football League. "I still have a love for the game in my heart, but it's a business," he said. "The toughest thing is to see guys I played with or against still in the league. I feel I should still be there, but I got tired of waiting. It was time to do something else."

Floyd is back at Michigan, working for Gittleson in the weight room at Schembechler Hall. He entered graduate school this fall and plans to get a Master's degree in education, with an eye toward becoming a college coach.

He was working out in the weight room one night two years ago when Jackson and Carr pulled him aside. They asked him if he would be willing to talk to senior B.J. Askew, who had bounced during his career between tailback and fullback. Heading into the 2002 season, the coaches recognized that the Michigan offense would be better if they could get Askew and junior Chris Perry on the field at the same time. That meant Askew had to move to fullback, as Floyd had done five years earlier.

Floyd agreed to talk to Askew. "I kind of paved the way for B.J.," he said. "I had been through it all, and I remember that it took me a long time to give in. I told that to B.J. I also told him that he was a much greater runner than I was, and that I knew he would be better at doing it than I was. After that conversation, he said he would do it. It all worked out fine for him and the team."

DENNIS FRANKLIN

The more Dennis Franklin listened to the debate last season about which two of the nation's three once-beaten college football teams most deserved to play for the Bowl Championship Series national championship in the Sugar Bowl, the less sympathy he could muster for any of them.

So what, Franklin now reasons sarcastically, if Southern Cal eventually had to "settle" for a berth in the Rose Bowl? At least the Trojans got to play in a bowl game. What if they'd had to endure the fate of the Michigan teams Franklin quarterbacked from 1972-74? Those three teams finished 10-1, 10-0-1 and 10-1—records that these days would easily qualify them for one of the major BCS bowls—but the Wolverines never played in a bowl game.

And, so what if the Trojans believed they were jobbed by the BCS formula? That was nothing, Franklin said, compared to the anger and frustration he and his teammates felt in 1973 after they learned that Big Ten athletic directors had voted to send Ohio State to the Rose Bowl after a 10-10 tie at Michigan Stadium.

"I played on three amazing teams at Michigan, and we got nothing for it," Franklin lamented. "There's no question that stunk. We got none of the bowl exposure that teams get today. You can make a living off the name you make for yourself in college these days. Not when we played. It's absolutely true: Timing is everything."

DENNIS FRANKLIN
Michigan letterman: 1972-1974

Position: Quarterback **Number:** 9
Hometown: Massillon, Ohio

All-Big Ten, 1973
Career passing: 153 of 294 for 2,285 yards, 18 TDs
Career rushing: 351 carries, 1,212 yards, 16 TDs

Franklin is as painfully familiar with that last statement as any athletic could be. During his senior year in high school in 1971, the NCAA passed and later rescinded a rule that would have allowed freshman to play. Had he been eligible, he believes he would have started at quarterback on Michigan's unbeaten 1971 team. The 1972 team was ineligible to play in the Rose Bowl because of the Big Ten's no-repeat rule, the '73 team was sidelined by the athletic directors, and the '74 team lost a 12-10 heartbreaker at Ohio State in the season finale.

The members of the '73 team remain bitter about the athletic directors' vote, Franklin says, particularly toward Michigan State. According to stories published at the time, MSU cast its vote for the Buckeyes, but Franklin believes that the Spartans actually voted for themselves. Had the voting been evenly split, he says, the Wolverines would have gone to the Rose Bowl.

Some athletic directors said at the time that they voted for Ohio State because they believed the Buckeyes had a better chance to win the Rose Bowl. Why? Because Franklin had separated his shoulder in the fourth quarter of the tie with the Buckeyes and might have been unable to play in the bowl game. The athletic directors were wrong on that count: Franklin's shoulder healed in plenty of time. In fact, one TV station photographed Franklin throwing snowballs in his parents' backyard during Christmas break. Ohio State did represent the conference well in the Rose Bowl, however, clobbering Southern Cal, 42-21.

Franklin was familiar with tradition long before he got to Michigan. He grew up in Massillon, Ohio, and was an all-state performer for one of high school football's most storied programs. He and teammate Steve Luke visited Michigan, Ohio State, Southern Cal, Notre Dame and Wichita State (where a former Massillon coach was head coach). Franklin's first choice was USC until he learned that another incoming quarterback, Pat Hayden, was living at Coach John McKay's house while he finished his senior year in high school.

Luke wound up at Ohio State, but Franklin says he never got along with Coach Woody Hayes. "Bo (Schembechler) and Woody were similar in terms of coaching styles and being disciplinarians, but Bo was more accepting of me," he said. "Any time I talked to Woody, he would insist that I commit by a certain time. Bo said I could make up my mind whenever I wanted to. That made me feel more wanted than Woody. Bo's attitude was very relaxed and very accepting."

MSU might have had the last word off the field in 1973, but Michigan was easily the better team in the state on the field that season. The backyard rivalry was played in a downpour that season in Spartan

Stadium. Franklin says he is particularly proud of that game because the Wolverines never fumbled and he never had a bad exchange with his center. Meanwhile, the Spartans contributed mightily to Michigan's 31-0 win by fumbling five times. "I hated playing in the rain," he says. "The only thing worse was practicing in the rain. But Bo never cut a corner when it came to weather conditions. We had to get through the (practice) agenda, no matter what was going on outside."

Franklin was 0-2-1 in his career against Ohio State, and both losses came in Columbus. The Wolverines lost 14-11 in 1972 and 12-10 in 1974. "I was always pumped up for those games down there," he said. "I liked playing there. The Ohio State fans made a big deal about my being a traitor, but I never felt that way. It was exciting to confront that garbage. Those people there are crazy."

The Detroit Lions selected Franklin in the sixth round of the 1975 NFL Draft, and immediately moved him to wide receiver. He never got a chance to play quarterback, though Coach Rick Forzano put in a couple of option plays featuring Franklin that the Lions could run near the goal line. He played less than two seasons for the Lions, who released him after they fired Forzano. "The Lions never gave me a shot at quarterback, which was unfortunate," he said. "There was that stigma about black quarterbacks. You would have thought perhaps the Lions might take a chance with me being a local guy, but they didn't. It was frustrating."

After failing tryouts with San Francisco and Miami, Franklin returned to Detroit and took a job selling advertising spots for WWJ-AM radio and serving as color commentator on the station's broadcast of Michigan football games. He moved to advertising sales for WDIV television and then to Comcast cablevision, before moving to New York City to work for King World. After 13 years, Franklin left the advertising business. He moved to southern California, lives in Santa Monica and sells real estate for Ferraro & Associates in Beverly Hills. Single, he has a 23-year-old son, Kenneth, who is an aspiring actor.

Franklin finished eighth in the Heisman Trophy voting following his senior season, and he isn't joking when he says that much of his notoriety he gained that season was a result of the publicity he got the previous year because of his separated shoulder.

"The *Football News* had me on its cover before the season as the preseason Heisman favorite, but nobody else was pushing me," he said. "Michigan had two Heisman winners in the 1990s, and they did it with exposure on television. In my day, if you were on television twice, you were at the top of the heap. Nobody had more games on television than we did. Now they're on every week."

JULIUS FRANKS

Whether playing football, excelling in school or getting involved in his community, Julius Franks has always been in the forefront.

He was just the second African-American to play football at Michigan and the first to earn All-America honors for his play on the offensive line in 1942. He earned a degree in dentistry in 1951 and practiced for more than 40 years in Grand Rapids before an illness forced him to retire. He was a respected professional and community leader in west Michigan for decades, with a particular interest in serving the needs of area youngsters.

There were few college opportunities for black athletes during the late 1930s and early 1940s, so Franks did not aspire to attend college after an outstanding career at Hamtramck High School. But because he'd been named to the all-city team following the 1939 season, he was invited to attend the annual Michigan Football Bust in Detroit. "When I saw all the Michigan fellows who were graduating that year stand up and say why it was important to get an education and what it meant to go to Michigan ... I decided right then that was the school I wanted to go to," he said. "That's what got the ball rolling for me." Still, his future at Michigan was not guaranteed. It was only after university officials inter-

JULIUS FRANKS
Michigan letterman: 1941-1942

Position: Guard **Number:** 62/63
Hometown: Hamtramck, Michigan

All-American, 1942

viewed him several times and considered many letters of recommendation that they admitted him.

Franks is still regarded as one of the toughest offensive linemen in
Michigan history. His head coach, Fritz Crisler, later said Franks was one
of the hardest-working players he'd ever coached. Franks played sparingly as a sophomore in 1941, but he emerged as an All-American at right
guard in 1942. In fact, he and linemates Philip Sharpe, Albert Wistert,
Robert Kolesar, Mervin Pregulman, Bill Pritula and Elmer Madar were
such a physical unit that one local sportswriter nicknamed the line the
"Seven Oak Posts." Franks attributes the success of that line to the experience it had gained during his freshman season (1940), when that group
would scrimmage against a varsity team that consisted of stalwarts such
as Tom Harmon, Forrest Evashevski and Bob Westfall.

Franks distinguished himself in 1942 during a 28-14 win against
Illinois on Halloween. He battled all afternoon against Fighting Illini
standout Alex Agase, who in the mid-1980s would become a member of
Bo Schembechler's coaching staff. Franks said he and Agase have kidded
each other for years about who had the advantage over whom in that
game. "We'd go back and forth with that one," he said. "We would joke
that I was the little boy and he was the old man."

A promising career was cut short a year later, when Franks and
teammate Tom Kuzma contracted tuberculosis. The two shared a room
at University Hospital for 25 months as they recuperated. "It was tough
time for both of us," he recalled. "But all the coaches, players and fans
would visit and send us letters. There were some very loyal people."
Crisler was a frequent visitor. Franks said he will never forget that
Harmon came to visit while he was on leave from the Army Air Corps.
In the absence of visitors, the two players came up with creative ways to
pass the time, and that included betting on horse races. They managed
to do it because another of their frequent visitors was a local bookie.

His bout with TB would affect Franks for years. While he was in
dental school, he could only stay up for eight hours at a time before he
would retire to bed to study. It was a routine he had learned during his
hospital stay. Doctors encouraged him to practice dentistry in a smaller
town where he would not be required to work nights.

Four decades later, another disease would force Franks to give up
another of his passions: dentistry. He was stricken in 1992 by Guillain-
Barre, a rare disease that affects the nervous system. He was forced to
close his dental practice in Grand Rapids, Mich.

In those 40 years, however, Franks did much to impact the lives of
many people in the western part of the state. He joined the Grand

Rapids Junior Chamber of Commerce and eventually became its president. He served as a leader in the Urban League, the United Way, the American Red Cross, the Boy Scouts and the Rotary Club. He was appointed by Governor George Romney in 1964 to the Western Michigan University Board of Trustees, and he served in that role for three decades.

But he might be best remembered for his role in helping to develop the Auburn Hills subdivision in northeast Grand Rapids that would offer homes to African-American families. Franks proposed to three friends and business partners in 1962 that they purchase a 20-acre tract of land from the city for the development. It took four years for the men to realize their dream. By 1983, nearly half of the city's black population lived in the neighborhood of well-kept homes.

Franks was inducted in 1982 into Michigan's Hall of Honor, which is open to former athletes who "have achieved on and off the field over the course of a lifetime and whose character, community service and moral standards exceed the ordinary." Three years later, when Franks was presented a distinguished service award by the West Michigan Dental Society, he was recognized as "a man of quiet impact." Asked why he had been so extensively involved to serve others, he said he felt obliged to give something back to his community.

"I was always interested in helping kids, because people had always helped me," Franks said. "I came along during the Depression, and there weren't many kids going to college at that time. It was kind of rough. There were no scholarships at that time, so you had to work for room and board. Back then, people helped you get a job, and that was the important thing."

FRANK GUSICH

Michigan has produced three Heisman Trophy winners, as well as winners of the Doak Walker, Butkus, Jim Thorpe, Walter Camp, Chuck Bednarik and Bronko Nagurski awards. More than 100 Wolverines have been honored as first-team All-Americans. Nearly 400 have been named first-team All-Big Ten selections.

None of those awards, however, is as significant as being named a Michigan captain. That, coaches insist, is the greatest honor a player can receive because captains are chosen by their teammates.

Frank Gusich agrees. He was a member of Bo Schembechler's first three Michigan teams, helped the Wolverines achieve their stunning upset of top-ranked Ohio State in 1969, and played in two Rose Bowls. What he remembers most is being elected one of the captains of the 1971 team. Center Guy Murdock was the other captain.

"For me, when I look back, that was my greatest honor," Gusich said. "What I hung my hat on was that I was the leader of that team. It was easily my finest moment as a football player. It was my moment in the sun. There were so many good guys on that team. My class in the NFL Draft that spring had the most selections of any school. For me to be a captain of that team was great."

FRANK GUSICH
Michigan letterman: 1969-1971

Position: Defensive back **Number:** 14
Hometown: Garfield Heights, Ohio

Captain, 1971
Career defense: 85 tackles, 7 tackles for loss, 4 fumble recoveries, 2 interceptions
Top game: 7 tackles, 2 interceptions at Northwestern, 1971

Being part of the '71 team is another point of pride that Gusich shares with each of his teammates. That team was the only one of the 21 coached by Schembechler that finished unbeaten and untied during a regular season, though it did eventually lose a heartbreaker to Stanford in the Rose Bowl. "It's hard to believe that, as phenomenal a career as Bo had at Michigan, we were the only team to do it," Gusich said. "We always have golf shirts made up for our reunions that say: '11-0, first and only.' The thought has crossed my mind at times that we shouldn't wear those shirts because they are almost putting down our coach. That's not what we mean to do, and he takes it great. It's hard to imagine him not going undefeated some other time. The guy was a great coach."

Gusich's class was the last one recruited by Bump Elliott, in 1968. A star at Cleveland St. Ignatius High School, Gusich first had to decide whether he wanted to play at a big or small school. Once he determined that bigger was better, he chose Michigan over Ohio State and Nebraska because he believed it combined the big-time football he wanted with an academic program that was the equal of any school in the country.

Because freshmen were ineligible to play on the varsity, Gusich never got much of a sense of Elliott's coaching style. When he was home on Christmas break during his freshman year, he heard reports that Schembechler had been hired as the new coach. And he remembers people who were familiar with Schembechler's reputation as a disciplinarian and a taskmaster warning him: "Look out. Life is going to be tough." Those predictions were correct. "That first winter conditioning was the toughest thing I have ever been through in my life. I remember that in spring ball, because we took time off for final exams, we had to stay (on campus) for an extra week. It was a boot camp."

That spring also was one of significant change for Gusich. He'd been a fullback his first season, but when Schembechler and his coaches reviewed film of the two games the freshman team had played the previous fall, they decided Gusich had the speed, smarts and tenacity to be a defensive back. He eventually became the backup to classmate Thom Darden at the wolf (strong safety) position. The following spring, Darden was switched to free safety, and Gusich grabbed the starting wolf spot, a position he held for the next two seasons. As wolf, Gusich played mostly to the strong side of the offense because he was responsible for helping to stop the run. But he said he also enjoyed any opportunity he got to play in pass coverage.

Gusich chuckled when he was asked to describe his best game as a player, because he says the games that stand out are the ones in which he didn't play well. "You don't remember the games in which you grade out well compared to the games in which you screw up," he said. Gusich believes his best game was the '71 season opener at Northwestern: He had two critical interceptions during a 21-6 victory. His most embarrassing moment came in the next-to-last game of the season at Purdue, when he fell down attempting to cover wide receiver Darryl Stingley on what turned out to be a long touchdown pass play. The Wolverines needed a last-second field goal to pull out a 20-17 win that clinched the Big Ten championship.

The Wolverines concluded the season with a 10-7 win against Ohio State at Michigan Stadium, but lost 13-12 to Stanford in the Rose Bowl on a last-second field goal. That defeat capped what had been a miserable trip for the Wolverines, who were plagued by lousy weather and illness almost from the minute they arrived in southern California. Michigan had been ranked No. 4 heading into the game. Gusich said that even had the Wolverines won, the best they could have finished was No. 2 behind powerhouse Nebraska. The loss dropped Michigan to No. 9 in the final Associated Press poll.

"That loss was a huge disappointment," he said. "It was the biggest game any of us had ever played in, and it was gone in the blink of an eye. We had a good enough team, but we didn't play as we were capable, and we lost a crazy game. What can you do? But I like to look at it another way: How many people would have given their right arms to be in that game?"

Gusich graduated the following spring with a bachelor's degree in business administration, and he considered enrolling in the business school to get his master's. But Schembechler arranged for him to interview with two friends from Cincinnati who owned the Midland Company, and they immediately hired Gusich. He worked for Midland until 1997, when the company sold the division of which he was vice president. He left the company that year and attempted unsuccessfully for nearly four years to purchase his own company.

The son of one of the men who first hired Gusich in 1972 asked him to return to Midland in late 2001. He now works as executive vice president of MG Transport, the company's barge division along the gulf coast from Florida to Texas and along the lower Mississippi River. Gusich lives and works in New Orleans.

Just after he returned to school after the Rose Bowl his sophomore year, Gusich met Linda Egner as he was walking across the campus Diag. She belonged to a student group selling tickets to a talk being given on the campus that week by activist Abraham Ribicoff. Gusich initially refused to buy a ticket, but when he met Egner again later the same day, he asked her if she wanted to accompany him to the talk. They dated through their final two years of college and were married in the spring of 1972. The couple has two sons: Mike, 27, who played football at the University of Illinois; and Brad, 25, who played lightweight football at the University of Pennsylvania.

The members of the '71 team remain a close-knit group, and teammates give Gusich much of the credit for that. He keeps tabs on former teammates and helps to plan reunions. That is part of his responsibility, he said. "I've always felt, after I was elected, that I was captain for life," he explained. "It was not just those 12 games. I'm always a leader, even 30 years later."

DAVID HALL

David Hall will never, ever say he was in the wrong place at the wrong time, but he recognizes that he might have had a better chance to start at quarterback for Michigan had he been born a few years later.

At 6-5, Hall was cut in the mold of most of the quarterbacks who have started for the Wolverines the past two decades. But Hall, now 41, played just before that, when Michigan was making the transition from an option-style attack to the pro-style offense the Wolverines use now. "I'm more like the guys who followed our group," he said.

Except that he was a marvelous athlete. A letter winner in football, basketball and track at Livonia Stevenson High School, Hall participated in all three of those sports at Michigan. And, while working on his master's degree in business administration from the University of Texas in the late 1980s, he emerged as one of the 10 best decathletes in the United States and competed internationally.

Hall never quite reached that pinnacle playing college football, but he achieved every Michigan quarterback's dream of playing in the Rose Bowl and he had one career start. Those are memories he will treasure forever. "I was disappointed that I didn't play more, but I went to Michigan with the goals of winning a Big Ten championship and going

DAVID HALL
Michigan letterman: 1982-1983

Position: Quarterback **Number:** 7
Hometown: Livonia, Michigan

Career passing: 33 of 63 for 331 yards, 4 TDs, 5 interceptions
Top game: 13 of 24 for 155 yards, 2 TDs, 2 interceptions vs. UCLA
in 1982 Rose Bowl

to the Rose Bowl," he said. "Getting the chance to play in the (1983) game fulfilled part of that goal. It was definitely a thrill."

Hall was a freshman on the 1980 Michigan team that gave Schembechler his first Rose Bowl victory, 23-6 against Washington. When the Wolverines returned to Pasadena two seasons later to face UCLA, Hall backed up classmate Steve Smith. He had played sparingly during the season, attempting just 14 passes. He prepared as if he would start the Rose Bowl, but he expected to play only if Michigan was either far ahead or far behind. He wound up with a much more important role than he imagined.

With the Wolverines trailing 7-0 in the second quarter, Smith ran an option keeper for eight yards and a first down, but his shoulder was separated when he was knocked to the ground by Bruins safety Don Rogers, and he left the game. Minutes later, UCLA took a 10-0 lead. Hall played in two series before intermission and completed one pass— a 10-yarder to Anthony Carter.

"That halftime was a whole different experience for me," Hall recalled. "I talked to Jerry Hanlon (then the quarterbacks coach) and Bo a lot about what we thought would work and what we had to do to get the offense moving. The coaches were very businesslike, and that helped a lot. There was no sense of panic."

The Wolverines marched 55 yards in the third quarter to cut the deficit to 10-7, and Hall completed the drive with a one-yard touchdown pass to fullback Eddie Garrett. The Bruins answered with a touchdown drive of their own to regain their 10-point advantage.

Hall's inexperience proved costly in the fourth quarter. With nine minutes remaining and the Wolverines pinned deep in their end of the field, Hall tried to squeeze a pass to Carter between a linebacker and a safety. The linebacker, Blanchard Montgomery, was supposed to cover running back Lawrence Ricks, but he anticipated Hall's pass, stepped in front of it and return the ball 11 yards for a touchdown that put the game out of reach.

"That was the crucial play and a crucial mistake," said Hall, who later tossed a four-yard touchdown pass to fullback Dan Rice. Hall finished the game with 13 completions in 24 attempts for 155 yards.

Hall made his one career start the following season, in the home opener against Washington State. The temperature on the field during the game exceeded 100 degrees, and Hall recalled that both teams had difficulty maintaining their energy and intensity. Though not known as an option quarterback, Hall scored the only touchdown of his career on a keeper late in the game. The Wolverines won, 20-17. A week later,

Smith, now fully recovered from the shoulder injury that had knocked him out of the Rose Bowl, returned as the starter.

Hall played one season (1981-82, his sophomore year) on the Michigan basketball team. He played in 12 games and scored against Eastern Michigan and against Purdue. It was enough to earn him a letter in that sport. "I lettered in three sports at Michigan, and that's something I'm very proud of," he said.

He also participated in track and field during all but his sophomore season. He competed indoors in the high jump and the high hurdles, and he threw the discus during the outdoor season. But his best event was the decathlon, and in 1985 he set a school record in the event that stood for eight years. "I liked the challenge of doing 10 different events," he said. "I was pretty fast, but not the fastest. I could throw the discus well, but not the farthest. I did well because I love the challenge of staying disciplined and mentally focused over two days."

With a background in economics, finance and accounting, Hall now provides expert testimony and economic analysis for a national firm in Denver, where he has lived the past 10 years. He and his wife, Ronette, a graduate of Oakland University, were married in 1993. The couple has three daughters: Kathryn, 8; Julia, 6; and Anna, 3.

"I went out to the Rose Bowl with my brother this year (2004), and it was a reminder again of what a thrill it was to play in that game," Hall said. "When you're in the game (as a player), it doesn't hit you that it's an experience you'll treasure for a lifetime. You're trying to execute the game plan. But, every time I go, the memories come washing back."

Where Have You Gone?

RICH HEWLETT

R ich Hewlett wonders occasionally how his Michigan career might have turned out if circumstances had been different. What if he hadn't been injured during his first career start as a freshman, late in the first half of the 1979 Ohio State game? What if he had gotten off to a better start the following season against Northwestern and at Notre Dame?

Such moments never last long. Hewlett, a two-sport star at Plymouth (Michigan) Salem High School, came to Michigan as an option quarterback. He finished his career as a defensive back and special teams player. But because he had made peace with the direction of his football career while he was still a player, Hewlett said, he was able to make the right choices in terms of his education and his career as an attorney, as well as his two remaining seasons as a Wolverine.

"I liked being a quarterback more than a defensive back because it was a much greater challenge," he said. "But, between playing quarterback and not playing or playing defensive back and at least getting on the field and being able to contribute, I enjoyed defense a lot more in that sense. I was just grateful I had the chance to play another position."

Hewlett was one of nearly a dozen quarterbacks looking to replace the departed Rick Leach when he reported to training camp as a fresh-

RICH HEWLETT
Michigan letterman: 1979-1980, 1982-1983

Position: Quarterback/Defensive back **Number:** 2
Hometown: Plymouth, Michigan

Career defense: 42 tackles, 3 pass breakups, 1 fumble recovery
Top game: 7 tackles, 1 interception vs. Indiana, 1983

man. B.J. Dickey and John Wangler were at the top of the heap, but Hewlett believed he was making a good impression until he injured a hamstring during two-a-days. That put him behind, but only temporarily. By the fifth game, at Michigan State, he'd made the travel roster. And, when Dickey was hurt midway through the season and Wangler stepped in as the starter, he was the backup. He played late during a blowout of Wisconsin in early November, but coaches resisted using him the following weekend during a 28-10 loss at Purdue – in part, he believes, because he was a true freshman.

With the offense struggling and the Ohio State game looming, Michigan coaches decided to make a change at quarterback. Head coach Bo Schembechler and quarterbacks coach Don Nehlen met privately with Hewlett that Monday, and they asked him what his reaction would be if he was asked to start against the Buckeyes. "I said, 'Hey, that would be great!'" Hewlett recalled. "I told them I was confident and I believed I could do the job." The two coaches asked Hewlett not to say anything to the team, because they wanted to make certain the change would work.

Hewlett began to work out that afternoon with the No. 1 offense and his practice time steadily grew during the week. On Thursday during the team meeting, Schembechler informed the rest of the team that Hewlett would start. "It was a senior-ladened team, and a lot of guys were surprised," he said. "I remember that seniors like Curtis Greer and Ron Simpkins were very supportive. Wangler was their guy. I think it was tough for them to see some young kid starting in that big of a game."

Because he was naïve about what he was getting into, Hewlett said, he was more excited than nervous about his first start. He threw an interception early, but the offense was moving the ball well. Even when the Wolverines were stopped near the goal line on one series, he was not discouraged. He admitted he was probably a half-step cautious because he was afraid of making a mistake, but he gained confidence with each series. He was certain that he could get through the first half and make some necessary adjustments at halftime, he and the offense would play well in the second half.

He never got that chance. As he was being sacked on one play in the second, one of his shoes caught in the artificial turf, tearing ligaments in his ankle. Trainers frantically tried to immobilize the ankle with tape so he could continue to play, but he could not run or make the cuts necessary to run the option. After losing 18-15, Michigan accepted a bid to the Gator Bowl, where Wangler seriously injured his knee. Hewlett was in a cast and on crutches for the next month and did not play in the bowl game.

The quarterback race changed dramatically the following spring. Dickey was gone, Wangler was hurt, and several others had quit. That left Hewlett and walk-on Brad Fisher as the only two quarterbacks on the roster. Again, he was No. 1. Again, it didn't last long. Michigan opened the following season against Northwestern, but the Wolverines were forced to scrap much of their game plan because the field was soaked from a torrential downpour the previous night and that morning. They squeaked out a 17-10 win against the Wildcats.

The offensive struggles continued the following weekend at Notre Dame, and Schembechler replaced Hewlett with Wangler when Michigan fell behind in the first half. Wangler rallied the Wolverines with his passing. The Wolverines lost 29-27 on the game's final play, but Wangler was back as the starter. In a surprising move, Michigan coaches then decided to scrap the option in favor of a power running and passing attack. The Wolverines lost the following week to South Carolina, but, with Wangler now at the controls, they never lost again that season.

Hewlett expected that he would get another crack at starting in 1981, but before the start of summer camp, defensive coordinator Bill McCartney told him he had one of two choices: He could back up redshirt freshman Steve Smith at quarterback or he could try playing on defense. That meant sitting out his junior season to learn a new position, so he could play in his fourth and fifth seasons. "That (redshirt) year gave me a little balance that I didn't have my first two years, and I was old enough to appreciate it," he explained. "It was at a critical juncture in my career. One, I wanted to make sure I got my degree. My grades needed to improve, because previously I had put a lot more emphasis on football. I wanted to take the time to do that. Two, I just wanted to play. I didn't care where. So, I said yes."

He split time his junior season practicing with the defensive backs and the quarterbacks, just in case a rash of injuries forced him to return to his former position. During his fourth season, he played mostly at short cornerback and free safety. He played some strong safety, too, as a fifth-year senior. He never started more than one or two games at any of those positions, but he was back on the field. He also played on special teams. "My view was, I tried to take pride in coming to practice and playing hard, being ready to play, and playing when I was needed," he said.

With a Michigan degree in hand, Hewlett went to work as a production control and scheduling manager for General Motors in its Chevrolet division less than a week after playing in the 1984 Sugar Bowl. That fall, he started law school at the Detroit College of Law.

Continuing to work full time and going to school at night, Hewlett completed law school in 3 1/2 years. He immediately went to work for the firm of Butzel Long, first as a summer intern and then full time in 1988. He has been a partner since 1997, and he joined the firm's Ann Arbor office in February, 2003. His area of expertise is construction law and litigation, and he handles business disputes and contract matters.

Hewlett's wife, Chris, is also a Salem High and Michigan graduate, but, because she is two years his junior, they were only acquaintances while in school. She also is an attorney. They discovered in 1989 that their respective law firms shared the same office building in Detroit, and they began dating not long afterward. They were married in 1991. The couple has two sons: Jeffrey, 10, and Joseph, 8. The boys' birthdays are two years and a day apart.

Hewlett chose Michigan over Alabama, and he also considered Notre Dame and Tennessee. He said he has no regrets about his decision.

"What I view now as some of my successes are not measured in terms of statistics and games started," he said. "I view it in terms of the friends I made and the relationships I built. I think that's probably how most of my teammates felt about their experiences, too."

Where Have You Gone?

KEN HIGGINS

Any time he watches a Michigan football game these days, Ken Higgins recognizes that he was a little ahead of his time. He would have fit right into the wide-open passing offenses of today's game that feature four- and five-receiver sets. Instead, he played at Michigan during the mid-1980s, when the Wolverines were making the transition from a predominantly run-oriented attack to one that was more balanced.

"I was the second-string split end every season," he said. "That would mean a lot of playing time today. Then, we still ran out of a lot of double-tight-end formations."

Higgins isn't complaining. When he got opportunities to play, he invariably made the most of them. He got plenty of mileage out of his career: He averaged 19 yards a catch on 36 career receptions.

Nor does Higgins wish he was playing today. That's evidenced by the fact that he passed up a fifth season of eligibility to begin classes at Harvard Law School. "I could have gone to law school at Michigan and played a fifth season, but I chose Harvard from a pure school standpoint," he said. "It has the strongest name recognition. It was hard to pass that up. My parents and two of my brothers went to Michigan, so I would have gone there even if I had not played football. I was always

KEN HIGGINS
Michigan letterman: 1985-1986

Position: Split end **Number:** 31
Hometown: Battle Creek, Michigan

Academic All-American, 1986
Career receiving: 36 catches, 685 yards, 1 TD
Top game: 8 catches, 165 yards at Wisconsin, 1986

focused on my education. Four years of football was great, but moving on (to Harvard) was the right thing to do."

His emphasis on school work was evident during his undergraduate years. Higgins was named a first-team academic All-American his senior season. He is one of just 17 players in Michigan football history to earn that distinction.

In some respects, Higgins's college football career was a strange and frustrating one. He was pressed into service as a true freshman after two players were suspended, and he was one of only three freshmen who made the travel squad. He expected to get increased playing time in 1984 as a sophomore, but instead sat out the season as a redshirt. "It felt like a step backward," he said, but admitted, "In retrospect, it was a good year because I focused on what I had to do to improve and to get playing time." The '84 season was frustrating in another respect: The Wolverines finished 6-6, becoming the only one of Coach Bo Schembechler's 21 Michigan teams not to have a winning record.

After catching just three passes total in his first three seasons, Higgins emerged as a reliable receiver in 1986, his senior year. He caught at least one pass in each of the Wolverines' 13 games, finishing with 33 catches for 621 yards and a touchdown. His longest career reception was a 51-yarder—for his only career touchdown—that season at Indiana.

Two games that season stand out for Higgins.

The first was the Big Ten opener at Wisconsin, when Higgins made his first career start for the injured Paul Jokisch and caught eight passes for 165 yards in a 33-6 win. Both totals were career highs. "It was a big deal to me to start, and it was my biggest game," he said. "Because of that game, I went from being an unknown to getting some attention. Personally, I felt that all the work I had put in had paid off. It was great to play and do well."

The other was the Rose Bowl, even though the Wolverines lost 22-15 to Arizona State. "Part of it is the history of the game, and part of it is that it's an incredible place to play," he explained. "You're out there in the late afternoon on a sunny day on one of the most immaculate fields you will ever play on. There is just huge energy in that game because, when you think about it, that's your No. 1 goal every year." Michigan led 15-3 early in the second quarter, but eventually lost the momentum. "Once the game turned, it was one of the only games I ever played in where I felt we couldn't get anything done," he recalled. "I felt like they were three steps ahead of us the whole game."

Higgins was recruited out of law school by a former Michigan basketball player, Bill Fraumann, to become a business associate in a

Chicago law firm, where he worked for four years before moving to Minneapolis in 1994. After working for a law firm there for nearly two years, he decided he wanted to try something different. He began work as an attorney specializing in merger and acquisition work for the investment banking firm of Piper, Jaffray and Co., and has since moved into the company's business unit, P.J. Ventures.

Higgins and his wife, Laura, also a Michigan graduate, have been married 15 years. The couple has two daughters, Laine and Sutton. The family lives in the Minneapolis suburb of Wayzata.

"I took a lot out of football that is still helpful," Higgins said. "One of the things Bo taught was that you prepared so thoroughly that, when you went out on the field, you never felt nervous. Another thing—and I'm not sure Bo gets enough credit for this—he was one of the best managers of people I have ever seen. Once I got a little older, I realized that everything he did had an objective."

Not long after the start of summer practice his freshman season, Schembechler began calling Higgins "Pinky." Higgins thought his head coach was making fun of him because he was so skinny. With the help of his younger brother, he eventually figured out why Schembechler chose that nickname. Turns out, Schembechler liked to give players nicknames derived from baseball, and Higgins's brother discovered while flipping through the 1984 World Series media guide that Pinky Higgins was a shortstop who played for the Detroit Tigers and the Boston Red Sox. "I asked Bo once I found out, and he told me that was where the nickname came from," he said. "Before that, he would never tell me."

Where Have You Gone?

DOUG JAMES

Doug James grins any time he remembers the good fortune and timing that brought him to Michigan as a football player. Though he insists he was the least athletically gifted of his 27 scholarship classmates, he had as memorable a career as any of them. He played four positions—middle guard on defense; right tackle and both guard spots on offense—and was elected team captain as a senior.

"When I was 13—and I almost remember the conversation as if it was yesterday—I told my dad that I was going to play football for Michigan," James said. "I have no idea how I arrived at that, but it happened. It is still hard for me to believe I ever played there. I guess everything aligned, and it happened."

What makes that story all the more difficult to believe is that James grew up and played football in Louisville, Kentucky, not exactly a Michigan recruiting hotbed. But he was interested in Big Ten schools because a former DeSales High School player, Bubba Paris, was having success at Michigan. It also helped that his high school coach, a Chicago native, had Big Ten connections. His recommendation meant a lot to Michigan coaches.

"I used to joke that I wasn't big, but at least I was slow," he said. "I had a pretty good understanding that to be good, I had to understand

DOUG JAMES
Michigan letterman: 1981-1984

Position: Guard **Number:** 73
Hometown: Louisville, Kentucky

Captain, 1984
Career defense: 32 tackles, 5 tackles for loss, 1 sack

the game and what my limitations were, so I had to be smart about how I played. I tried to learn as much about everything as I could. I knew what everyone was supposed to be doing on any given play.

"Bo (Schembechler) used to say that I had the worst body in the history of Michigan football. I would always answer him: 'If I had the worst body, why did I play so much for you?' And he would say: 'Because I'm a heck of a coach.' I don't think he was joking around."

What Schembechler did appreciate was James's willingness to take on new challenges. He played middle guard his first two seasons (1980-81) before switching in the spring to offense at the request of Michigan coaches. He started the 1982 season at right guard, but after four games coaches asked him to move to right tackle. He finished that season and started every game in 1983 at that position. When he decided to play a fifth season, coaches again asked him to move, this time to left guard. He started nine games at that position before a serious leg injury he sustained in practice ended his football career.

"I don't think it was that difficult for me to switch positions, because I just wanted to play," he said. "I think a lot of guys, when they're being recruited, envision themselves only at a certain position. I just envisioned playing football. When the coaches came to me in the spring of my third year and wanted me to move to offense, I was not that receptive, but I was smart enough to get the message. They did not have plans for me any more on defense."

James said he had highlights at every one of his positions. He played well in the 1981 Notre Dame game at Michigan Stadium, and he recorded a key sack the following week to preserve a 21-16 win against Navy. On offense, James said he was probably best suited to play guard because he had the size and quickness to block linebackers, but he believes he had his best games in 19 consecutive starts as a tackle. He wonders how good he might have been had he spent his entire career at just one position.

James switched from right guard to right tackle the week of the Michigan State game in 1982. He did not start that game but played most of it. He started the following week at Iowa, he lined up across from Mark Bortz, who would go on to play for the Chicago Bears. James believes he played one of his best games as a collegian that afternoon.

James hadn't planned to return for a fifth season. He'd promised his high school sweetheart, Patty, they would marry as soon as he completed his degree, which he was on track to do in four years. Schembechler tried to discourage James because there were no married players on the team. James was insistent that he'd only return if the coach could live with the fact that he was married. Schembechler reluctantly agreed.

The 1984 season was a tough one for Michigan, which finished 6-6. The Wolverines started 3-1, including a win against defending national champion Miami (Florida), but a rash of season-ending injuries, including one to quarterback Jim Harbaugh at Michigan State, depleted a thin lineup. James said he did not play well in a 31-29 loss at Purdue in early November, so he was eager for a chance at redemption in practice the week before the final home game against Minnesota. But when he became tangled with several defenders on a screen pass, he broke his leg and dislocated his ankle. His career was over.

"I still catch grief from Bo's guys about being the captain of a 6-6 team, but I tell them that I made them look better," he said. "It was disappointing, but at the same time, you don't always win in life. We had some struggles, but we could have overcome them if it hadn't been for the injuries. We probably were a 9-3 team if Harbaugh hadn't been hurt."

James began work as an announcer for Michigan football games on WTRX in Flint in the late 1980s, and he later took a job with the station in sales. He returned to Louisville as a sales manager for a group of radio stations there, and he worked for 10 seasons as a color commentator on radio broadcasts of University of Louisville football. He now works as director of sales for Radio One, which owns six Louisville-area radio stations, and he serves as a color commentator on local television broadcasts of Louisville football.

He and Patty celebrated their 20th wedding anniversary this year. The couple has three daughters: Amanda, Beth, and Katie.

"If there is anything that came out of my Michigan experience, it's that ordinary people sometimes get extraordinary opportunities," James said. "I was glad I was able to take advantage of mine."

Where Have You Gone?

RON JOHNSON

Ron Johnson likes to joke that he came to Michigan for all the wrong reasons. Rival coaches—he won't say from which schools—offered him money above and beyond a scholarship and all sorts of additional perks when they recruited him out of Detroit Northwestern High School. They promised him he would start at running back as a sophomore, and they assured him he could enroll in an easy physical education curriculum so he was sure to remain eligible.

Michigan offered none of that, he says, particularly the guarantee of playing time. Coach Bump Elliott was candid with him: Johnson might play as a sophomore, but he'd be behind seniors Jim Detwiler and Carl Ward on the depth chart. Plus, as far as school work was concerned, Johnson wasn't interested in a physical education degree. He started out in the engineering school and wound up finishing in the business school.

"I'm not sure why I didn't go for those other things, considering I was a young man, but something about Michigan got to me," he said. "For whatever reason, I was impressed with Bump and his sincerity. I still think of how blessed I am today because I made that choice."

Johnson's career turned out just as Elliott had predicted. He played a little bit at halfback in 1966, his sophomore season, but he made the travel squad because he could also fill in at defensive back. He emerged as the featured running back during his junior and senior seasons, however, and he delivered what, at the time, were the two best individual rushing performances in school history. His 347-yard effort in 1968, his

Billy Taylor

Dennis Franklin

Doug Skene

Gene Derricotte

Hercules Renda
Photo courtesy of Jim Cnockaert

Ken Higgins

**Bill Daley (right) with artist Duane Bryers at Daley's
Minneapolis art gallery**

Carl Kreager

Bob Timberlake (lower left), his wife Bobbi and their family

Dave Hall and his family (from left): wife Ronette, Julia, Anna and Kathryn

Jim Betts and his family (from left): Evan, Eric and wife Marty

Larry and Dawn Sweeney

Doug James and his family (from left): Amanda, Katie, Beth and wife Patty

Rich Hewlett and family (clockwise): wife Chris, Jeffrey and Joseph

Ron Johnson and some teammates at 35th reunion of 1968 team

The Wistert brothers (from left): Albert, Alvin and Francis

John Kolesar (left) with Bill Kolesar
Photo courtesy of Jim Cnockaert

Michael Taylor
Photo courtesy of Jim Cnockaert

Tom Slade
Photo courtesy of Jim Cnockaert

Tony Branoff
Photo courtesy of Jim Cnockaert

Bruce Elliott
Photo courtesy of Jim Cnockaert

Carlitos Bostic
Photo courtesy of Jim Cnockaert

Cecil Pryor
Photo courtesy of Jim Cnockaert

Dana Coin
Photo courtesy of Jim Cnockaert

Frank Gusich
Photo courtesy of Jim Cnockaert

Gordon Bell
Photo courtesy of Jim Cnockaert

J.D. Carlson
Photo courtesy of Jim Cnockaert

RON JOHNSON
Michigan letterman: 1966-1968

Position: Running back **Number:** 40
Hometown: Detroit, Michigan

All-American, 1968. Big Ten MVP, 1968. Captain, 1968.
Career rushing: 477 carries, 2,417 yards, 25 TDs
Top game: 31 carries, 347 yards, 5 TDs vs. Wisconsin, 1968

senior season, against Wisconsin remains the best in school history. His 270 yards against Navy in 1967 now ranks fourth on the all-time list.

After gaining just 44 yards on 12 carries his sophomore season, Johnson began 1967 by gaining 82 yards in a win against Duke and 30 yards in a last-second loss at California. The following weekend, he ran wild against Navy, averaging 10.4 yards per carry. The Wolverines suffered another close loss, but Johnson's performance did wonders for his confidence.

"That was probably the game that really made me realize that I had something special," Johnson said. "I can remember my runs so distinctly. I got through the line and had to make a decision, either cut in or cut out, and it seemed like every decision I made was the right one. That was the game where everything opened up. My whole attitude and confidence level changed. I felt I was a pretty good running back. My nervousness dropped dramatically. I just went out and played on instinct, just like I did in high school."

The 1967 team finished 4-6 overall, but enough talent returned the following season to give Michigan a crack at the Big Ten title. With Johnson providing much of the legwork—he rushed for 19 touchdowns and 1,391 of the team's 2,270 yards—the Wolverines ran off eight straight victories after losing the opener to California. That set up a showdown at Ohio State for the championship. Johnson had six games of 100 or more yards, including a 205-yard effort at Duke. He saved his best performance for his final game at Michigan Stadium.

Michigan needed a win against Wisconsin in the home finale to make the game at Ohio Stadium the following weekend a truly meaningful one, but it trailed at halftime. As the teams headed up the tunnel to their respective locker rooms, a Wisconsin receiver taunted the Wolverines, yelling that mighty Michigan was nothing. That fired up the Wolverines, who rolled to a 34-7 win. Johnson, who spent most of the game following the blocking of fullback Garvie Craw, carried 31 times for 347 yards and five touchdowns. Both totals are still single-game school records.

Asked if he sensed just how many yards he was gaining as the game wore on, Johnson replied: "Heck no. I took myself out of the game after the first play of the fourth quarter. While I was sitting on the bench, our statistician came down from the pressbox and asked me if I knew how many yards I'd just rushed for. When he told me 347 yards, I couldn't believe it.

"Our main focus in that game was to win to play Ohio State. That's what my thoughts were. But the way we ran the ball that day, that's when the game becomes fun. Ask any running back. The more you carry the ball, the more you get into a groove. Once you're in that zone, you want the ball on every play. That's how I felt that game."

Johnson's spirits and those of his teammates didn't remain high very long. A week later, Michigan was manhandled 50-14 by an Ohio State team that would go on to win the Rose Bowl and the national championship. Johnson says the Wolverines were out of sync the entire game, and it seemed as if every break went the Buckeyes' way. Ohio State coach Woody Hayes attempted to add insult to injury in the game's closing seconds when he tried a two-point conversion following his team's last touchdown.

"We all cried like babies in the locker room," he recalled. "The junior and sophomores assured us they would take care (of the Buckeyes) next year, but it didn't matter to the seniors. We had as good a team as Ohio State, but it was one of those days. That was the frustrating thing. That was the biggest game of our careers, and to know that we didn't give our best was devastating."

The Cleveland Browns selected Johnson in the first round of the NFL Draft the following spring, and he helped the team reach the championship game against the Green Bay Packers that season. But he was unhappy playing behind Leroy Kelly, so the Browns traded him to the New York Giants, for whom he played six more seasons. The Giants never reached the playoffs during Johnson's career with them. "After that, I lost all my passion for the game," he said.

Johnson was hired as an institutional salesperson by a Wall Street investment firm in the late 1970s, but he'd always been interested in purchasing a fast-food restaurant. He tried to buy three McDonald's franchises during his one season in Cleveland, but the deal fell through. Seven years after he retired from pro football, he decided it was time to become his own boss. He approached several hamburger chains, but he was told he could only buy one restaurant at a time. When he asked Kentucky Fried Chicken company officials about their franchise opportunities, they told him he could open as many restaurants as he wanted to as long as they were doing well.

The 56-year-old Johnson now owns KFC restaurants in New Jersey, where he lives with his wife of 34 years, Karen. He also has restaurants in Michigan and Tennessee. He has two children: Christopher, a senior at Boston College; and, Allison, a junior at Georgetown University.

"Having come out of Michigan's business school, I felt I had more potential than one franchise," he said. "I did not want to become a glorified store manager. My sights were set pretty high."

DICK KEMPTHORN

Wherever Dick Kempthorn played football, winning followed. His Canton McKinley High School teams finished 16-2-2 and won a state championship during the two seasons he started at quarterback and linebacker. He played six games—all wins—at Miami of Ohio before being accepted into the United States Merchant Marine Academy during World War II.

Kempthorn later played on three Big Ten championship teams at Michigan from 1947-49, during which the Wolverines finished a combined 25-2-1, walloped Southern Cal in the 1948 Rose Bowl and won a pair of national championships. He was an All-Big Ten and All-America performer during his senior season, after which he was voted the team's most valuable player.

Former Michigan teammates believe they know exactly why he was such a success on the football field: No player they'd ever played with or against was more single-minded and ferocious than Kempthorn. Pete Elliott, who played two seasons on defense with Kempthorn, once recalled: "I truly have not seen a more reckless but effective player in my life. My biggest fear on a sweep was not the opponent, but Dick. He would hurt you more coming from the inside to help with the tackle

DICK KEMPTHORN
Michigan letterman: 1947-1949

Position: Linebacker/fullback **Number:** 38
Hometown: Canton, Ohio

Career rushing: 63 carries, 250 yards, 4 TDs

than any opponent. He hit everyone near the ballcarrier, and extremely hard. I went to great lengths to convince him I was a sure tackler."

Kempthorn grins at such recollections, because he admits that was the way he played the game. "It was a case of, you can be a nice guy off the field, but you have to quit when you hit the field," he said.

Kempthorn did not play football his freshman year in high school. He played trumpet in the McKinley marching band, and his mother, an accomplished musician, hoped he would take up music. Admitting he must have missed out on the family's musical gene, Kempthorn gravitated to what came naturally, football. He was captain of the McKinley team his senior season, after which Big Ten schools lined up to offer him scholarships.

Instead, he enlisted in the naval reserve and eventually learned he would be admitted to the U.S. Merchant Marine Academy in San Mateo, California. Between the time he graduated from high school and shipped out in the fall of 1944, he attended Miami of Ohio for two months and played six games for the Redskins under Coach Sid Gillman. Those games cost Kempthorn a year of eligibility at Michigan.

He spent six weeks at the academy and was sent to sea for experience. He spent the remaining months of the war serving as an engine cadet aboard a cargo ship, the USS Wild Hunter, which participated in the invasion of the Phillippines.

When Kempthorn came home on furlough after the war, he was encouraged by a former McKinley teammate, Stu Wilkins, to visit Michigan. Kempthorn told Michigan coaches during his 1946 visit that he intended to return to the Merchant Marine Academy, but they convinced him to stay in Ann Arbor.

Kempthorn was a starting linebacker and a backup fullback on the 1947 "Mad Magicians" team, the last coached by Fritz Crisler. Kempthorn had early success as an offensive player, scoring a touchdown in the season opener against Michigan State on just his second career carry. He had a brief conversation later in the locker room with assistant coach Bennie Oosterbaan, who told him: "Big boy, they won't all come that easy. You haven't been hit yet."

Two weeks later in a 69-0 win against Pittsburgh, Kempthorn injured his knee and missed two games. When he returned, he realized that he could not perform many of the spinning movements required of a fullback in Michigan's intricate single wing. He had mixed success the rest of the season, but he did play well during a win at Wisconsin that clinched the Big Ten title and later in a 49-0 win against Southern Cal in the Rose Bowl.

The Wolverines handled USC so convincingly in the bowl game that The Associated Press took the unprecedented step of conducting a post-bowl poll, and Michigan passed Notre Dame in a vote of national sports editors. The Fighting Irish had been declared national champs in the final poll of the regular season. There would be no split decision a season later, as undefeated Michigan finished atop the AP poll.

Kempthorn believes the 1949 team was every bit the equal of its two predecessors, but it suffered back-to-back losses to Army and at Northwestern early in the season and finished with a 7-7 tie against Ohio State. "We should have gone undefeated in 1949, but it seemed that it was fate that we didn't," he said. "When we were at full strength, we were a good team." The Wolverines were hobbled in the game against Army. Star senior lineman Alvin Wistert played with an injury he'd suffered the week before, and junior halfback Chuck Ortmann left the game after being kicked in the head on the third play.

After Kempthorn played on three college all-star teams following his senior season, professional teams such as the Philadelphia Eagles and the Cleveland Browns of the All-America Football Conference sought his services. But the United States was again at war, this time in Korea, and Kempthorn re-enlisted, this time in the Air Force. He spent more than three years as a pilot, flying more than 100 missions in prop planes and jets. He earned numerous decorations, including the Distinguished Flying Cross, because of his bravery.

Kempthorn returned to Canton in 1953, and Cleveland Browns coach Paul Brown was eager to sign him to a contract. Brown sent assistant coach Dick Gallagher to the Kempthorn home. Gallagher was met at the door by Kempthorn's father, Jim, who turned the coach away without hearing his offer. "My father said I was the only son he had, and I was done playing football," he recalled. "He was not in good health, and if I wanted to take over the business, it was mine. Otherwise, he would have sold the business."

So Kempthorn went to work for the family Dodge-Plymouth dealership in Canton, and in 1965 he bought the business from his father. He has since expanded the business to two dealerships that feature 11 different brands of automobiles and trucks. He remains the company's president. His two sons, Eric and Jim, and his daughter, Dana, also work in the business.

"I feel very fortunate to have everyone here," the 77-year-old Kempthorn said. "I'm still working every day, because I enjoy it."

Where Have You Gone?

BILL KOLESAR

It occurred nearly 50 years ago, but Bill Kolesar can still vividly recall the block that ended his football career. To his astonishment, many Michigan fans remember the play, too.

"It's funny, but I get that a lot," he said. "I'll be talking about my career, and I'll mention what happened, and someone will say, 'I remember that play!'"

Michigan faced Michigan State at home in the second game of the 1955 season, and the Wolverines kicked off to start the second half. Kolesar, a senior, headed downfield hoping to level the Spartans' return man. Instead, he was leveled. As he closed in for the tackle, an MSU blocker—he's pretty certain it was Norm Masters, but teammates later told him it might have been Buck Nystrom—caught him in the legs with a crack back block. Kolesar says the collision knocked him five feet into the air, and he did a complete somersault before landing on the back of his shoulders.

He survived the rough landing OK, but the hit that put him there tore the medial collateral ligament in one of his knees. He underwent surgery the following week and never played another down for the Wolverines.

BILL KOLESAR
Michigan letterman: 1953-1955

Position: Tackle **Number:** 75
Hometown: Mentor, Ohio

"That was a tough thing, because I had waited my turn to be a starter," he said. "I always thought you waited for your turn. That's what you did for the sake of the team: You waited your turn. Looking back, I probably would have done things a little different. I would have been more aggressive going to a coach to get a chance (to play). I never did, because I expected my turn was coming."

When Kolesar was growing up, his home town of Mentor, Ohio, was a developing community east of Cleveland. It now boasts the state's largest high school. His coach was Lee Tressel, who would later coach at Baldwin-Wallace College. The families were close, and Kolesar used to babysit the older Tressel boys. He had left for college by the time the youngest son, Jim, the future Ohio State coach, was born.

Kolesar was Mentor's first big prep football recruit, and he had already committed to play football at Cleveland's Western Reserve College when two area Michigan alumni invited him to visit Michigan. He used to listen to Michigan games on the radio, but he never considered going there. In fact, until he was a sophomore in high school, he hadn't thought at all about going to college. "I conned my parents into buying me a car—a 1949 Ford—because I told them I was planning not to go to college," he said. "I changed my mind and switched to college prep classes. Up to that point, I had been taking basic curricula like mechanical drawing."

At Michigan, Kolesar played left tackle on Michigan's unbalanced offensive line. His position was similar to that of a pulling left guard. As a sophomore, he played behind Dick Strozewski and future All-American Art Walker. As a junior, he played behind Walker, who was a senior. Kolesar preferred defense to offense, but under the strict substitution rules of the day, most players went both ways. "If a player came out of the game, he had to sit until the last two minutes of the quarter," he explained. So, Kolesar waited for his opportunity to start. He was eager to improve his skills in practice by going against Walker, but Michigan coaches wouldn't let him after he knocked out Walker on a trap block during the spring game in 1954. "If the rules had been different, I would have gotten a lot more playing time than I did," he said.

Ironically, Kolesar never did start at left tackle for the Wolverines. He says coaches were interested in using a hotshot sophomore at that position in 1955, so he agreed to move to right tackle. He started the first two games before suffering the injury.

Kolesar says he will never forget the 1954 game at Ohio State, in part because it was the one time he played in his home state and part because he played against Ohio State All-American Jim Parker. "Being from Ohio, I wanted to stick it to them," he said. "We lost 21-7 down there. We did everything statistically but score." Earlier that season against Illinois, he caught running back J.C. Caroline from behind. "I had good speed for a lineman," he said. "I could beat our 100-yard dash man in high school for the first 20 yards."

Kolesar's knee had healed enough the summer following his senior season that he was able to try out with Ottawa of the Canadian Football League. The tryout lasted five days, until his knee buckled during a practice drill. Team officials had arranged to have a knee brace delivered to training camp, but it never arrived. "I said the heck with it," he said of his career. He returned to Michigan to complete the two classes he needed for his history degree. He considered applying to law school, but instead went into sales. He first worked for Shell Oil, then for Uniroyal in southern Ohio and Kentucky, and later for two discount store chains in the Cleveland area. He then worked 25 years for Georgia-based Enforcer Products, servicing hardware stores in northeastern Ohio, before retiring four years ago.

Kolesar and his wife, Joyce, who live in the Cleveland suburb of Westlake, celebrate their 47th anniversary this fall. They have four children: Scott, Anne-Marie, Doug, and John. All three boys played high school football. Doug was a punter at Miami of Ohio. John was an All-Big Ten wide receiver at Michigan. "One of the greatest feelings in the world is seeing your son play at your alma mater," he said. "You're on top of the world, especially if he does well."

As it turned out, the Kolesars and the Tressels were linked through several generations. One father coached the other. The youngest sons would face each other—in a way—years later in college football's greatest rivalry. John Kolesar had some of his greatest moments as a Wolverine against Ohio State. He caught four passes for 109 yards, including a 77-yard reception for a touchdown, to help Michigan defeat Ohio State 27-17 in 1985. The Buckeyes' defensive backs coach in that game was Jim Tressel.

Where Have You Gone?

JOHN KOLESAR

John Kolesar wonders how fans might remember his career had he made his biggest plays against, say, Northwestern rather than Ohio State. Would he still be regarded as one of the finest wide receivers in Michigan history?

"There's no question that the timing of plays is what makes people consider them great," Kolesar said. "You have to be in the right place at the right time. If I score against Illinois or Iowa, maybe I'm not remembered in the same way. But if you do something against Ohio State, you will live in infamy."

As many players from the state of Ohio did during their Michigan careers, Kolesar had a knack for delivering big plays against the Buckeyes. He caught four passes for 109 yards, including a 77-yard reception for a touchdown, to help Michigan defeat Ohio State 27-17 in 1985. Three years later at Ohio Stadium, he returned a kickoff 59 yards to set up a 41-yard touchdown reception with a little more than a minute remaining. That was the difference in a 34-31 Michigan win.

Even if Michigan fans have forgotten Kolesar's heroics, Ohio State fans most certainly have not. Kolesar, who recently moved back to his native Westlake, Ohio, knows this because the Buckeye faithful remind him about it constantly. "Everyone in Ohio still brings it up—those 1985 and 1988 games—and you can tell their blood pressure is rising just by looking at their faces," he said. "But, you know what, people down there respect me as a football player, so they'll buy me a beer. I

JOHN KOLESAR
Michigan letterman: 1985-1988

Position: Wide receiver **Number:** 40
Hometown: Westlake, Ohio

All-Big Ten, 1988
Career receiving: 61 catches, 1,425 yards, 12 TDs
Career long: 77-yard TD catch vs. Ohio State, 1985

appreciate that. People I went to high school with used to tell me: If Michigan had to beat the Buckeyes, at least it was Johnny doing it. Ohio State fans are very devoted to their school, but they respect good football."

No one who knew Kolesar's family history expected him to play for the Buckeyes. His father, Bill, had played for the Wolverines in the 1950s. Kolesar was such a Michigan fan growing up that he would fearlessly wear maize-and-blue shirts to grade school, even though the "10-Year War" between the teams of Bo Schembechler and Woody Hayes aroused great passions in his home state. "People were convinced I was pre-destined to go to Michigan," he said. "(But) that wasn't going to happen unless Michigan gave me a scholarship."

And that wasn't guaranteed. Kolesar had a good high school career as a running back, but only Stanford and North Carolina initially offered scholarships. Though he'd always refused to go to summer camps, he accepted an invitation to go to Michigan's the summer before his senior season. Michigan coaches suddenly became interested after he turned in the fastest 40-yard-dash time in camp. Schembechler eventually offered Kolesar the last scholarship remaining for the incoming 1985 freshman class.

Kolesar was the only running back recruited in his class, so he took every snap during the three days of freshman orientation practices before the varsity reported for training camp that August. On the last morning of freshman practice, Schembechler used to ask promising players to switch positions, with offensive players typically going to defense, and vice-versa. When Schembechler came to Kolesar, he poked him in the chest with a finger and said he wanted him to try wide receiver. The Wolverines lacked numbers at that position, and Kolesar made such an impression that he moved to third on the depth chart. "That meant that I was on the travel squad," he said. "I never played a down on the demonstration teams."

That didn't necessarily mean that Kolesar would play a significant role in the game plan. Because the Michigan offense then was much less diverse than it is now, much of the passing attack centered on passes to the running backs. "We hardly threw downfield except on third and forever," Kolesar said. He made his first start in the final nonconference game of that season against Maryland, but he never caught more than one pass a game through October. In a 3-3 tie at Illinois that November, Kolesar had single coverage all afternoon, but only one pass was thrown in his direction (he caught it). "It was embarrassing to look at the film the next day and see that," he said. "The next week, I caught four passes against Purdue."

Kolesar admits it would be easy to focus on the successful plays he made during his Michigan career, but he can't forget his mistakes. "That plays into my humility," he said. For instance, though he made two exceptional plays that helped Michigan beat Ohio State in 1988, he remembers that he dropped a pass earlier in the game.

Still, he doubts he will ever forget his last Ohio State game. After the Buckeyes scored to take a 31-27 lead, Kolesar took the ensuing kick-off three yards deep in his end zone and returned it to the Ohio State 49-yard line. Two plays later, after sitting out a play to catch his breath, he boxed out two Ohio State defenders to make the touchdown catch. "Scoring the winning touchdown in 'The Horseshoe' (Ohio Stadium) in my last game was really something special," he said.

Buffalo selected Kolesar in the fourth round of the 1989 NFL Draft, and he played two seasons for the Bills. He injured his knee in both seasons, and that forced him to wear a brace that hampered his speed and mobility. If the injuries hadn't prompted him to end his career, his disenchantment with professional football would have. "Pro football was highly different for me—the business aspect of it—and I didn't like it as much," he said. "There's a saying that in college you compete and in the pros you perform. Guys want to protect their longevity, so it seems they're more selfish. I felt that, considering where I came from, the NFL was a step down in terms of the quality of the people and the facilities."

Kolesar says he has lived the past decade in 10 different places, including stops in Los Angeles, New York City, Grand Rapids (Mich.) and the Washington, D.C., area. He has worked at a variety of jobs, all involving sales. He now works for Foundstone, a company that specializes in Internet security software services and education. He and his wife, Tara, have been married five years. The couple has three children: Filomena, Caden, and Jace. The family lives five minutes from his parents' home in Westlake, Ohio.

Though he made many memorable plays at Michigan, Kolesar refuses to judge his career solely on them. He prides himself on being a student of the game. For instance, during Michigan's 22-14 win against Southern Cal in the 1989 Rose Bowl, Kolesar took himself out of the game after Schembechler called for a post route that was better suited to Chris Calloway. As Kolesar had anticipated, the play went to Calloway for a touchdown.

"Fans remember the touchdowns and the big plays, but I pride myself on having done all the right things beforehand," he said. "I prepared myself mentally and physically to the point where I was in a zone. My level of performance in both those sectors is what I value."

Where Have You Gone?

CARL KREAGER

It could have been Chuck Ortmann, who punted an astounding 24 times. Or, it could have been Tony Momsen, who blocked a punt and fell on it in the end zone for what proved to be the game-winning touchdown.

But Carl Kreager's teammates insist that he is the real hero of Michigan's 9-3 win against Ohio State in the strangest game ever played in the series, the 1950 "Snow Bowl" game in Columbus. Kreager was the center for Michigan's single-wing offense and special teams, and his on-target snaps enabled the Wolverines to endure some of the worst weather conditions imaginable and eventually triumph against the Buckeyes.

The day before the game, the worst blizzard since 1913 paralyzed the Midwest and Northeast. Record low temperatures gripped the entire eastern half of the nation. At least nine inches of snow fell on Columbus Saturday morning before kickoff. By game time, the temperature was near zero degrees and the snow was swirling around Ohio Stadium, driven by northwest winds of up to 30 miles an hour.

Amazingly, the brutal conditions never fazed Kreager. "I could have shut my eyes and the ball would have hit my hands," Ortmann said about his center. "The ball never missed where my hands were."

CARL KREAGER

Michigan letterman: 1949-1950

Position: Center **Number:** 56
Hometown: Detroit, Michigan

But Kreager, now 75, believes his contribution to the victory tends to be exaggerated because Ohio State's center played so poorly during the game. "(Ohio State punter Vic) Janowicz had to play shortstop back there," Kreager recalled. "We blocked two of their punts because the ball was not getting back to the punter. That made it look like it was more difficult. I can't say I played a great game, but I knew I had to get the ball back there. That's where all the practice paid off. We practiced and practiced getting the ball to the right spot."

By the end of the 1940s, most college football teams had scrapped the aging single wing in favor of the T-formation, in which the quarterback lined up under center. But Coach Bennie Oosterbaan, like his predecessor, Fritz Crisler, used the single wing because it relied on quickness and deception rather than size and brute strength. The playbook consisted of double-reverses, laterals, crisscrosses, quick hits and spins.

No player was asked to do more in Michigan's single wing than the center, who had to master seven different snaps. Depending on the play and where it was going, Kreager might snap the ball hard or soft, high or low, directly to one of the halfbacks or away from him to provide a lead of a yard or two.

"If the ball wasn't in the right spot, we were in trouble," Kreager said. "When you see teams today use the shotgun (formation), the center never looks back. When I played, you had to keep your head down to see where you were centering the ball. We ran from an unbalanced line, so the center pulled on some plays. And there was no such thing as a long snapper. The center did everything. You were on the field when we received the kickoff, and you might be on the kicking team. You were on the punt teams. It was a more direct game then in terms of participation."

Kreager had a number of college options after a successful football career at Detroit Cooley High School. His father wanted him to study engineering at Purdue, but Kreager chose Michigan because of its football reputation and because it was close to home. He enrolled in 1947, just in time to participate on the demonstration teams in practice against Crisler's "Mad Magicians," who won the Big Ten championship and clobbered Southern Cal in the 1948 Rose Bowl. A season later, he played some at linebacker on the Wolverines' Big Ten and national championship team. He earned letters in 1949 and 1950, but he didn't start at center until his senior season.

Though his performance in the "Snow Bowl" stands out, Kreager says he played his best game earlier in the season during a 7-7 tie at Minnesota. One of the Golden Gophers' defensive tactics was to hit the

Michigan center as often as possible and from every direction in an effort to throw off his snapping. Kreager never flinched. "I took a beating, and I was bleeding from someplace any time I came out of the game," he recalled. "But I played a great game in terms of what I had to do."

Kreager was drafted by Green Bay, but he turned down the Packers' offer of $5,000. He taught and coached for a year at Dexter (Michigan) High School. But a Packers assistant coach was persistent, and he eventually convinced Kreager to sign for $7,500 salary and a $1,000 bonus. He played three games with the Packers before a head injury ended his football career.

Kreager and Ortmann worked as manufacturer's representatives in Detroit during the offseason selling nonferrous metals. But after the company's owner convinced Kreager he had the potential to do and earn more, he took a job with a large development company. After 11 years, he left to start his own building and development business. Now retired and living in Florida, he still owns a number of apartments in Michigan and two mobile home parks in Florida, is the primary owner of a retirement community in Petoskey (Michigan), and is a partner in six other apartment developments. "I still keep the wheels turning instead of just retiring and walking out the door," he said.

Recently, Kreager read former President (and Michigan center in 1934) Gerald Ford's biography, *Time and Chance*, and he was amazed by the similarities in their college careers. Both men came from poor backgrounds. Both played center. Neither started until his senior season. Ford was approached by the Packers at the conclusion of his Michigan career; Kreager was drafted by the same team.

"It brought back a lot of memories," he said.

Where Have You Gone?

JOHN MORROW

John Morrow grew up with Michigan football. The backyard of his parents' Henry Street home in Ann Arbor backed up to Stadium Boulevard, so the family parked cars there on football Saturdays during the fall. Morrow and his buddies occasionally would hop the fences at Michigan Stadium to sneak into games. One of his best friends was Fritz Crisler's son, Scott. Morrow attended and played football at Ann Arbor High School (now Pioneer High), just across the street from the stadium.

There was little question where Morrow would go when it came time for college. His father, a long-time Prudential insurance agent, had turned down several opportunities to transfer within the company because he hoped that each of his four children would attend Michigan. All of them did.

Given that history, no one would have been surprised had Morrow had a life-long dream to play football for the Wolverines, but he didn't. It wasn't until he had success at Ann Arbor High—he started at offensive and defensive tackle for two seasons for the undefeated Pioneers—that he considered playing for the Wolverines.

"My only intention was to go to Michigan to get an education," he said.

Photo provided by Bentley Historical Library

JOHN MORROW
Michigan letterman: 1953-1955

Position: Tackle **Number:** 78
Hometown: Ann Arbor, Michigan

Morrow did much more than that. He played center for most of his sophomore season (1953) and then finished his career at right tackle. He played center for 11 seasons in the National Football League—four in Los Angeles after being drafted by the Rams in 1956 and seven in Cleveland. He was a Pro Bowl performer in 1963, and he helped the Browns win the NFL championship in 1964.

Because few scholarships were available, Morrow, like most of his teammates, took on just about any job he could to make ends meet. As a freshman, he sold programs at the stadium. Later, he ran the kitchen for his fraternity and scraped the ice at the Coliseum in preparation for and between periods at Michigan hockey games.

After senior captain Dick O'Shaughnessy was hurt during the '53 season, Morrow stepped in to play center in Coach Bennie Oosterbaan's single-wing offense, as well as linebacker on defense. Playing center was a difficult challenge, he said. "You're making a direct snap and there are five different spots you can put the ball, so you couldn't keep your head up," he explained. "The center was sort of lost at the start of a play, because you were a second or so behind a shifting defense. It was a slight disadvantage in terms of blocking."

Morrow said that many of the memories of his college career have faded after five decades, but he recalls that at 218 pounds, he was one of the heaviest guys on the team. All-America tight end Ron Kramer played at 220 pounds. "If you got any heavier than that, the coaches put you on a diet," he said. Morrow also remembers the longest road trip of his career, to play Washington in 1954. The Wolverines won that game 14-0. Later than season, he blocked an Earl Morrall punt in a 33-7 win against Michigan State. "The games tend to blur a little bit," he said. "What I remember most is the camaraderie at practice. I was fortunate to have played with a great bunch of people. We just loved to play the game."

The Rams selected Morrow in the 28th round of the 1956 Draft, and he quickly became a fixture at center. Morrow suffered a knee injury that required surgery during the 1959 season, and, after the Rams fired Sid Gillman as head coach, they swapped centers with the Browns, sending Morrow to Cleveland for Art Hunter. "That was definitely a move up," he said. "I played with guys like Jim Brown and Paul Warfield, and I roomed with Lou Groza. My years in Cleveland were great."

Morrow took a mix of education and business classes during his four years at Michigan, and he left for the NFL a few credit hours short of his degree. He completed two spring semesters at Michigan while he played in the pros, thinking that would be enough to finish up. He then was informed he needed one more three-hour speech class to get his diploma. "I never did go back," he admitted.

He held a variety of off-season jobs while playing in Los Angeles, including selling real estate. When he got to Cleveland, he began a store manager training program with Goodyear, but he made several contacts that eventually got him a job in the packaging industry. After he retired from the NFL, he moved to Wisconsin, where he worked 19 years for the Menasha Corp. and 18 more for Weyerhauser.

Morrow met his future wife, Gail, when both attended a summer college music camp at Interlochen in the northern part of Michigan's lower peninsula. Back at Michigan, he literally ran into her rounding a corner at Angell Hall and bumped some books out of her hands. The couple dated for five years before marrying in 1956. They have one daughter, Johnna, who lives in Minneapolis.

"So many things have changed in 50 years," Morrow said. "Football is so different in so many ways. I was lucky to have played with a great bunch of guys, and I would suspect the guys playing now feel the same way about their teammates. That's probably the one thing that hasn't changed."

Where Have You Gone?

CHUCK ORTMANN

R eflecting on his life from the perspective of more than seven decades, Chuck Ortmann says he realized pretty much every one of his boyhood dreams.

Ortmann intended to play college football, as did his idol, Tom Harmon of Michigan. Ortmann wanted to play in the Rose Bowl, and he planned to play professional football. He also hoped to have a high school sweetheart whom he would eventually marry.

"Every dream of mine was answered," said Ortmann, who grew up in Milwaukee during the Depression. "It was a hard life as I grew up, but it was a simple life. I did not have a computer or a television. I listened to a small radio, and I stretched my imagination. Memory became the biggest thing of all."

Ortmann's greatest memories might have been of Harmon, and he kept several scrapbooks full of newspaper stories and photographs of the All-America halfback who won the Heisman Trophy in 1940. Ortmann played the same position at Michigan a decade later, and while he did not earn as many individual honors, he accomplished things Harmon did not. He played on four Big Ten championship teams. He also made two trips to the Rose Bowl and played in the 1951 game.

From right: Richard Kempthorn, Leo Koceski and Chuck Ortmann.

Photo by Francis Miller/Time Life Pictures/Getty Images

CHUCK ORTMANN
Michigan letterman: 1948-1950

Position: Halfback **Number:** 49
Hometown: Milwaukee, Wisconsin

All-Big Ten, 1949
Career rushing: 273 carries, 676 yards, 6 TDs
Career passing: 127 of 314 for 2,078 yards

Surprisingly, Ortmann didn't believe he was good enough to play at Michigan until a fellow classmate, who had close friends living in Ann Arbor, suggested he consider going to school there. He received scholarship offers from hometown Marquette University (when that school sponsored football) and from Bear Bryant at Kentucky. The University of Wisconsin wanted him so badly that the governor of the state sent a limousine to his house to take him to his recruiting visit. Unfortunately for the Badgers, he'd left earlier that same morning to visit Ann Arbor.

"My high school coach would say: 'Chuck, if you pick Michigan, you're picking the best. After you graduate, people will know you and remember you,'" he recalled. "I made the right decision."

Ortmann arrived in Ann Arbor in the summer of 1947 with six dollars in his pocket. He quickly became homesick, but he had to stay because he needed two more dollars to pay for the Greyhound bus fare back to Milwaukee. When he lined up with the seventh string on the first day of freshman practice, he was convinced he had no chance to play college football. He was embarrassed because, though he'd played halfback in high school, he didn't know where to line up in Michigan's single-wing formation. But before long, he was running on the demonstration team.

"I had to make a key block on one particular play, and I had to face (senior defensive end) Lenny Ford," he said. "Many years later when I was with the (Pittsburgh) Steelers and we were playing the (Cleveland) Browns, the right defensive end was Lenny Ford. On one play he came in unopposed and dropped me like a toothpick. He told me after the game it was lucky I had played for Michigan, because he took it easy on me. He could have put a shoulder into me and knocked me out for life."

Ortmann broke into the starting lineup at left halfback for the Michigan State game his sophomore season after starter Gene Derricotte was injured. When Derricotte was healthy enough to return to the lineup, he started only on defense. As Harmon had done, Ortmann played both offense and defense during most of his career.

He also punted, as Harmon did, and he is assured a noteworthy spot in Michigan football history because of his punting exploits during the 1950 "Snow Bowl" game in Columbus. In blowing snow and bitter cold, Ortmann punted 24 times to tie a modern NCAA record. "You and I would not have gone outside to get the newspaper on a day like that," he said. "But here we were, trying to play football." Michigan did not get a first down, gained only 27 yards rushing and did not complete a single one of its nine pass attempts, but it triumphed 9-3 to earn a trip to the Rose Bowl.

Michigan players grabbed for every bit of clothing they could find that afternoon in an effort to stay warm. Amazingly, only one pair of gloves was available: a fine deerskin dress that belonged to graduate assistant coach Dick Kempthorn. He offered them up for the cause. The logical person to wear the gloves was center Carl Kreager, but he refused because he worried they would hamper his snapping. Ortmann initially refused to wear the gloves, too, but, because he never came off the field, he soon realized it was better to wear gloves than have frozen fingers.

After graduation, Ortmann played one season for the Pittsburgh Steelers, who then waived him. He played in an all-Big Ten backfield the following season for the Dallas Texans, but he reinjured the ankle that had bothered him for much of his senior season at Michigan, and he was finished with football. He was hired by a Chicago company that sold nonferrous metals. The company was owned by another former Wolverine, Ernie Vick. Ortmann retired and moved to Savannah, Georgia, in 1991.

Ortmann also married his high school sweetheart, Betty. He'd seen her one day walking down the main staircase at school and immediately fell in love with her. They have been together since. They raised four children and have seven grandchildren.

Ortmann was inducted earlier this year into Michigan's Hall of Honor, but he doesn't consider himself to be one of the great football players in school history. "When fans start talking about putting an all-time Michigan team together, I think they're wrong to pick someone from the old era," he said. "I led the Big Ten one season with 750 yards running and passing. A guy like John Navarre has as many yards and passes in a game as I did in a season. Guys I played with were as good as they come, but nothing like the players today. Dominic Tomasi was a lineman at 5-8 and 180 pounds. They have cheerleaders that big today."

Where Have You Gone?

DAVE PORTER

Dave Porter had a decision to make his senior year at Lansing (Michigan) Sexton High School that few athletes today ever face. He was a good football player, but an even better wrestler. He was offered football and wrestling scholarships. Michigan was one of the schools willing to let him compete in both sports, if that's what he wanted to do.

"I ended up on a football scholarship, but I could have competed in either sport, or both of them," he said. "It was up to me, and I decided to do both. There were other guys on the football team who played basketball or baseball. The football coaches had no problem with that as long as you were busy doing something."

Porter probably was more heavily recruited as a wrestler than he was as a football player. He was a three-time state wrestling champion, winning at 180 pounds as a sophomore and at heavyweight as a junior and senior. As he looked up from a workout one afternoon early in his senior season, he noticed Iowa State wrestling coach Harold Nichols sitting in the corner watching him. The following spring, he was called down to the main office because Oklahoma State coach Myron Roderick had stopped by the school to talk with him.

He could have attended either of those collegiate wrestling powerhouses on a scholarship, but he'd decided early on to go to Michigan.

DAVE PORTER
Michigan letterman: 1966-1967

Position: Defensive tackle **Number:** 70
Hometown: Lansing, Michigan

Career defense: 46 tackles, 4 pass breakups, 2 fumble recoveries
Top game: 11 tackles at Minnesota, 1967

First and foremost, he wanted to study architecture. Second, he wanted to stay close to home. Third, Michigan football coach Bump Elliott and wrestling coach Cliff Keen encouraged him to compete in both sports. "The sports really didn't overlap much," Porter said. "You'd play football until Thanksgiving, and then there was a break and exams. Our first wrestling meet every year was the Midlands Tournament in late December."

Porter was a two-year varsity football starter at Sexton, playing both offensive and defensive tackle. He played offensive tackle on the freshman team and during his sophomore season at Michigan, but he moved to defensive tackle for his final two seasons.

He played one of the best games of his career in 1966 at Michigan State, where he recorded seven tackles, recovered a fumble and broke up a pass during a 21-7 loss to the top-ranked Spartans. One of the offensive linemen he occasionally faced during that game was guard Mike Bradley, who also was on the MSU wrestling team. They had competed against each other on the wrestling mat long before they bumped helmets on the football field.

Michigan's base defense at the time was a 5-2, in which the three interior linemen operated out of a four-point stance and sacrificed their bodies to give the two inside linebackers room to make the tackle. For reasons Porter cannot explain, the Wolverines switched to a 4-3 look in 1967 for a late October game at Minnesota. That allowed the linemen to play in a three-point stance, and Porter responded with what he considers to be the best game of his career. "I don't know why the coaches did it. Maybe it was just time to make a switch," said Porter, who collected a career-best 11 tackles in the game. "It sure made things a lot more enjoyable. That enabled you to move around. You'd get a hit on an offensive lineman, then get off of him to look for the running back or the quarterback. You weren't just in the pile trying to grab anything you could get your hands on."

Porter, who was elected to Michigan's Hall of Honor in 1985, left a more lasting legacy at Michigan with his wrestling exploits. A three-time All-American, he won NCAA championships at heavyweight in 1966 and 1968 and finished third in 1967. He had a 13-1 record in three NCAA tournaments. Those 13 wins are the sixth best total in school history and the most among Michigan wrestlers who, because of NCAA eligibility rules, could not compete as freshmen. He was the Big Ten champion at heavyweight in 1966 and 1967.

Porter had hoped to compete in the Olympics, either in 1964 or in 1968. He missed the '64 Games because he broke his foot his senior season at Sexton. He could not compete in the '68 Games because he'd signed an NFL football contract that voided his amateur status.

The Cleveland Browns selected Porter in the ninth round of the 1968 Draft, but he tore a tendon in his foot that prevented him from playing even in a preseason game. Interestingly, though he was drafted as a defensive lineman, the Browns almost immediately moved him to offensive tackle. Early in rookie camp, he volunteered to play center and long snap, because the center the Browns had drafted out of Florida State did not report. "If I could have run, I would have made the team as a center," he said. Porter also reported to the Browns' training camp the following summer and did play in some preseason games, but he did not make the final roster.

Porter's dream of becoming an architect didn't last long, because he soon realized that the afternoon classes he needed to take conflicted with football and wrestling practice. Instead, he went into education, eventually getting a degree in physical education and earning a teaching certificate.

After graduation, he taught briefly at Lansing (Michigan) Waverly High School and at a high school in New Jersey before accepting a job as a physical education teacher at Grand Ledge (Michigan) High School in 1970. He has been there ever since. He is now 58. He has never been married.

At first, Porter also coached the Grand Ledge wrestling team. He gave up all coaching five years ago. His last Grand Ledge coaching assignment was the tennis team.

"I think I coached just about everything at the school," he said.

Where Have You Gone?

CECIL PRYOR

Cecil Pryor heard the rumblings, and he didn't like them. Bump Elliott was about to be re-assigned within the Michigan athletic department, which meant the football team would soon have a new head coach. Pryor, who was heading into his senior season, hated that he would have to prove himself to a new regime. Besides, the old coaching staff had promised to showcase him during the upcoming season, to position him for postseason honors and, later, for the National Football League draft.

It was a traumatic time for Pryor and his teammates, and it was about to get even more so. The entire dynamic of the football program changed the day Bo Schembechler was hired as the head coach. Compared to the low-key, personable Elliott, the intense Schembechler was like a cold slap in the face, and he immediately began reshaping the Wolverines into a team that mirrored his personality.

The new coach's demanding off-season regimen prompted many players to quit. Pryor considered that option, but realized he had no choice but to stick it out. Pryor had never been afraid to speak his mind, however, and that put him at odds often with his new coach. Schembechler twice kicked Pryor off the team, once in the spring and again during summer drills. "Bo and I are friends now, but back then we

CECIL PRYOR
Michigan letterman: 1968-1969

Position: Defensive end **Number:** 55
Hometown: Corpus Christi, Texas

Career defense: 106 tackles, 9 tackles for loss, 3 pass breakups, 4 fumble recoveries **Top game:** 15 tackles vs. USC in 1970 Rose Bowl

didn't get along," Pryor said. "I think I made Bo uneasy. I used to question a lot of stuff, and he didn't like that. He came in real aggressive, trying to set the tone for the rest of his career. I understand that now, but I didn't then. And, if you ask him, Bo will tell you that he was harder on our team than he was on any one that came after us."

A native of Corpus Christi, Texas, Pryor was heavily recruited by schools in the Big Eight and Pacific-8 conferences and by small schools in his home state. Because big Texas state schools didn't recruit black players at the time, Big Ten teams such as Michigan State and Minnesota were able to stock up with quality players. Though Michigan recruited few players from his area, Pryor liked the school. There were several reasons. Most important, a former coach, Y.C. McNease, was one of Elliott's assistants. Pryor also liked Michigan's combination of strong academics and athletics. Finally, he'd grown up watching the Michigan-Ohio State game. It was the one Big Ten game he knew he could watch on television every year.

"I also thought it would be fun to play football in a cooler clime," he said. "When I was growing up, we used to play night games where it would be 90 degrees and sweltering. But I had a rude awakening when I got to Ann Arbor. The morning of the Illinois game my freshman year, the coaches and managers came pounding on our doors in South Quad around 6:30, telling us we had to get up to help shovel snow out of the stadium. I hadn't bargained for that."

It would not be the last time he felt that way. Pryor was recruited as a quarterback, but he was immediately switched to linebacker. He was stunned, but he admits most teams then liked to recruit quarterbacks and move them to other positions. For instance, the entire secondary on the 1969 Michigan team was composed of former quarterbacks. Pryor played defensive end when the Wolverines used a 4-3 scheme and a standup outside linebacker when they went to a 5-2 look.

Pryor played some of his finest games against Michigan State, because many Spartans were Texans. In fact, so many MSU players were friends that he spent a lot of time on the East Lansing campus. That's where he met his future wife, Jan. "State was always my red-letter game," he said.

Pryor says he and his teammates will always remember their stunning 24-12 upset of top-ranked and defending national champion Ohio State in 1969 at Michigan Stadium. The seeds of that win had been sown at Ohio Stadium the previous season, when Ohio State coach Woody Hayes tried a two-point conversion following the Buckeyes' last touchdown in a 50-14 win.

"You have to understand, that (upset) had been building for 365 days," Pryor recalled. "They beat the crap out of us the previous year. This had been building like a volcano, and all of a sudden it's eruption time. We knew they couldn't beat us that day. We knew that someone would make a play, sell the farm, or do something to prevent them from winning. After a quarter and a half, Ohio State knew they couldn't win, too.

"That was probably the greatest game I ever participated in my life, and I had been playing football since the fourth grade. It is the game I remember most from my career. Mind you, my biggest rival personally was Michigan State. But that (Ohio State) game stands out more than any other."

Pryor had mixed success as a professional player. Selected in the fifth round of the 1970 NFL Draft by Green Bay, he was cut by the Packers and later by the Philadelphia Eagles. He played three seasons for the Canadian Football League's Montreal Alouettes before returning to the United States to play for the Memphis Southmen of the fledgling World Football League. The Memphis franchise, owned by Canadian businessman John Bassett, was the WFL best capitalized team, so players were paid well. Pryor earned $100,000 a season—considerably more than many NFL stars made. But, when the WFL folded after two seasons and the NFL refused to grant Bassett an expansion franchise, Pryor's pro career was over.

Pryor returned to Ann Arbor to complete his degree in education, and he was working on a master's in guidance and counseling when he was approached by Bob Vlassic, another Michigan alumnus. With Vlassic's financial backing, Pryor began O.E. Financial, a company that leased capital equipment. For 10 years, it was one of the most successful minority-owned companies in the state. But Pryor sought an even better opportunity, and in the late 1990s, he entered Ford Motor Company's dealer training program. After a four-year apprenticeship and another year of managing company-owned franchises, he bought the Ford dealership in Jackson, Michigan. He has owned the dealership for 11 years. Pryor also served as a member of U-M's Board in Control of Intercollegiate Athletics for 12 years.

He and Jan have been married 29 years, and they live in Ann Arbor. They have three daughters: Melissa, 26; Cecilia, 24; and, Hillary, 21.

"My Michigan career was a very key experience," he said. "I don't regret any of it, because without any of those things occurring, I might be in a completely different situation today, and I am comfortable in my situation."

HERCULES RENDA

Coach Bennie Oosterbaan pulled Hercules Renda aside and asked him to wait around after class. It was the final session of the spring football coaching class Oosterbaan was teaching, and Renda was just days away from getting his Michigan diploma. After the other students had left the room, Oosterbaan asked Renda: "Coach (Fritz) Crisler asked me to ask you if you would be interested in being an assistant coach this fall for the freshman team?" Renda nodded. "It won't pay very much," Oosterbaan continued. "Only $200." Renda just grinned and thought to himself: "I'll give you $200 to do that!"

There's no telling what his lifetime of Michigan football experiences might be worth to Renda now. Each of them, he would insist, is beyond price, and who could argue? If any former player embodies the history, tradition and spirit of Michigan football, it is Renda.

He played in Coach Harry Kipke's final season (1937) and on Crisler's first two Michigan teams. He played for two seasons in the same backfield with eventual Heisman Trophy winner Tom Harmon, and he played against two other Heisman winners, Iowa's Nile Kinnick and Minnesota's Bruce Smith. He was on the first Michigan team to wear the winged helmet. As a member of Crisler's staff in 1940, he coached with

HERCULES RENDA
Michigan letterman: 1937-1939

Position: Halfback **Number:** 17/85
Hometown: Jochin, West Virginia

1938-39 statistics: 11 carries, 69 yards, 2 TDs; 2 interceptions

Oosterbaan and future Michigan State coach Biggie Munn and occasionally helped athletic director Fielding H. Yost.

Renda, who turned 87 in September, likes to say he has spanned all three centuries of Michigan football. He got to know members of the 1898 team—the one that inspired Louis Elbel to compose the school's fight song, "The Victors"—when they gathered in Ann Arbor in 1938 for a reunion. And he was on the field at Michigan Stadium in November with generations of other former players to help inspire the 2003 team to a victory over Ohio State.

"When I look back, I have done things I love to do," he said. "As a player, I didn't understand the significance of the Michigan program as it was from the very beginning when Yost came (in 1901). (But) can you imagine how everything has fallen into place as it relates to my life? Athletics has been my life. I often tell people that I have not worked a day in my life. I've had my ups and downs, but in reality, I have no complaints. Just think of the privilege I've had, and it grows more meaningful with each day that goes by."

Renda's unusual first name suggests that he is a man of tremendous strength and stature. The strength part is accurate enough: When Renda offers one of his huge hands in greeting, he has a vise-like grip. His size is deceiving, however. At 5-3 1/2, Renda is one of the smallest players in Michigan history, but it once took seven Minnesota defenders to bring him down on a play in the 1937 homecoming game. His name was given to him by his mother, who while pregnant with him had read a book about the mythical Greek hero, Hercules, and was inspired by his extraordinary feats of strength and courage. That explanation wasn't sexy enough for some local sportswriters of the day, who suggested that Renda had been named after Hercules blasting powder, the explosive his father used to mine coal.

Renda was one of nine children, five girls and four boys. His parents were first-generation immigrants from Italy, and his father moved the family around until he settled in the hills of West Virginia near Charleston. Renda's father and two older brothers worked in the coal mines. One brother, Frank, was an organizer for the fledgling United Mine Workers union.

At East Bank High School, the same school that later produced basketball star Jerry West, Renda was a good athlete, but not a great one. The best athlete in school was Renda's closest friend, Roland Savilla, who stood 6-4 and weighed more than 200 pounds. Friends called them "Mutt and Jeff"—a reference to the popular newspaper comic strip. Savilla was heavily recruited, particularly by Lon Barringer, a Charleston businessman who was Kipke's close friend. Savilla agreed to attend

Michigan, but only if Renda could come along. In Renda's 1936 high school yearbook, Savilla wrote: "College classmates, I hope." Renda jokes that he rode Savilla's coattails to Michigan. "I was a tag-along," he said. "Otherwise, I probably would have gone to work in the mines like everyone else."

Savilla eventually became a fixture at tackle for the Wolverines. Renda started three games his sophomore season at halfback. He scored a touchdown on a pass from Stark Ritchie in the season opener against Michigan State, but the Spartans prevailed 19-14 on a late touchdown. With the arrival in 1938 of Harmon and Paul Kromer, "The Touchdown Twins," Renda's playing time diminished, but he relished every opportunity he got to play football.

Considering the positions they played, Renda and Savilla wore jersey numbers that would be considered strange in today's game. Renda wore No. 17 as a sophomore, but he switched to No. 85 for his final two seasons. Savilla wore No. 29. "Up to 1937, numbers were given out helter-skelter," he said. "I'm not sure why running backs were given such high numbers, but I never thought much about it at the time."

Renda left Michigan to serve in the army air corps during World War II, and he rose to the rank of master sergeant while serving as a physical training specialist. He later re-enlisted in the air force reserves, and he eventually retired as a lieutenant colonel.

He married his beloved Norma Jean in 1945 and moved to Flint, where he was an assistant football coach and junior varsity basketball coach at Central High School. There, he coached future Michigan quarterback Rick Leach's father and uncle. He was the head football coach at Pontiac High School from 1948-52. After teaching for several more years at two local junior high schools, he became athletic director and head track coach at Pontiac Northern when that high school opened in the late 1950s. He retired in 1982.

He still lives in the house across the street from Northern High School that he and Norma Jean built in 1962. The couple adopted and raised two children: Steven, who lives in Dallas; and, Joanne, who lives close by in Pontiac. Norma Jean died in 1998, a month before the couple's 53rd anniversary.

Asked if he has a favorite Michigan moment, Renda replied: "Every moment was the best moment. I don't know that I can pick one out. I appreciated the total experience of being part of the greatest football program in the country. For whatever reason, I keep going back to the words, opportunity and God-given ability. I was able to put those two things together to play at Michigan."

Where Have You Gone?

ROB RENES

Rob Renes shrugs his shoulders any time he's asked to recount the best game he ever played at Michigan. He doesn't have what he considers a good answer, he says, because he doesn't think of his college career in those terms. He doesn't differentiate one game from another because he believes every game was his best.

"Sure, there are moments that stand out," he said. "My first start (at Colorado in 1996) was a big game. Being on the 50-yard line in the Rose Bowl after we won the national championship, that was very special. Leading the band in Miami after my last game (the 2000 Orange Bowl) was special, too. But—and I think this is true for most of us—every game I played was the best I could play. I always gave it my all."

Renes carried the same attitude and work ethic into the classroom. While he hoped to play football professionally, he recognized that at 6-1, he was undersized for a defensive lineman. He wanted to be ready in case his football career ended with his final Michigan game.

That effort and diligence paid off in 1999, when he became the fourth Michigan player to earn first-team All-America honors both for football and academics. The others were Bob Timberlake (1964), Jim Mandich (1969) and Stefan Humphries (1983).

ROB RENES
Michigan letterman: 1996-1999

Position: Nose tackle **Number:** 58
Hometown: Holland, Michigan

All-American, 1999. Captain, 1999.
Career defense: 149 tackles, 24 tackles for loss, 5 sacks, 3 fumble recoveries
Top game: 8 tackles vs. Notre Dame, 1997

"Any time you're recognized for your ability or an accomplishment, that's something you're going to take a lot of pride in," Renes said. "School was always a top priority with me—and it's something Coach (Lloyd) Carr always talks about—so I think the academic (honor) overshadows the athletic. But I think the two really lent themselves to one another. I knew I would never be the best player I could be if I was not the best student I could be. So, from the day I stepped on campus, I wanted to be the best in anything I did."

Renes, a native of Holland, Michigan, was recruited by a number of Big Ten schools and Notre Dame, but he'd always been a Michigan fan. He committed to the Wolverines the minute Coach Gary Moeller offered him a scholarship in 1994, and he didn't waver the following spring after Moeller resigned. Renes said he believed what he'd always been told by the Michigan coaches who'd recruited him: That no one person was bigger than the program.

After redshirting his freshman season, Renes saw spot duty in every game during the 1996 season, and he started at Colorado. He was the only defensive lineman to start all 12 games during the 1997 national championship season, and he did not miss a start in his final two seasons, either.

"The '97 season definitely stands out because of the success of the team," he said. "It was an important year in terms of understanding what my role on the team was and what my role would become. I learned as I went along. That was true for a lot of guys, because that defense was relatively young. But we played well collectively. Looking back on that season, I don't remember ever being uptight or thinking that we had to do something special. We went into every game expecting good things to happen. That was one of the big marks of our defense that season."

Because it returned many players from the previous season, the 1998 team had high expectations, but back-to-back losses at the start of the season quickly dashed them. Renes remembers that season, not in terms of the early disappointment, but because of the way the Wolverines regrouped for the remainder of the season. There was more disappointment in 1999, when back-to-back midseason losses to Michigan State and Illinois cost Michigan a chance to play in the Sugar Bowl for a shot at the national championship. But the Wolverines rallied to win at Penn State and against Ohio State to finish the season and then twice overcame 14-point deficits to defeat Alabama in the Orange Bowl, 35-34 in the first overtime game in school history.

"That senior season was a great time in my life," said Renes, who was one of the captains of the '99 team. "Those two losses were tough, but we put them behind us. That's one of the reasons Michigan has been consistently good over the years. I never thought about woulda or coulda or shoulda. It was still a great season."

Renes finished his career with 151 tackles, including 24 for losses and five sacks, and he recovered three fumbles. He was a semifinalist for the Lombardi Award following his senior season, and he was Michigan's Big Ten Medal of Honor winner that year. He earned degrees in German and social studies from Michigan. He is now working on a master's in counseling.

Though he hadn't expected to play professionally, Renes gave it a shot after both he and roommate Josh Williams were drafted in 2000 by the Indianapolis Colts. His dream was short-lived, however, because he broke his back before the team's first preseason game and was placed on injured reserve. After teaching for a year in the Saline, Michigan, schools, he attempted to make a comeback with the Colts, but his back injury again flared up. He never played a game in the NFL.

Uncertain what to do next, Renes obtained a real estate license and worked as a realtor in Ann Arbor for a year. He decided to return to teaching, and he is a middle school geography and social studies teacher in the Reeths-Puffer school district near Muskegon. He is an assistant coach for the high school varsity football team, and he is the defensive coordinator this season.

"I knew when I played at Michigan that I had to be the strongest and the fastest I could be, and that attitude lent itself to the classroom," Renes said. "I knew that I couldn't just show up on Saturday and count on my God-given ability to succeed. The success I had in football created a mentality that I could be a success in anything I tried. I had to work hard to make the most of my ability. I recognize that was an advantage for me."

Where Have You Gone?

LAWRENCE RICKS

L awrence Ricks never had a doubt about his choice of Michigan as an academic institution, but he questioned at times early in his freshman season whether he'd made the right choice in terms of football. The Wolverines were loaded with good running backs. He wondered whether he would ever see the field.

"Once you realize you can play, that's when you stop worrying about stuff like that," he said. "I played some as a freshman, but I really took off during practice for the (1979) Gator Bowl and during spring practice. I came to the realization in the spring that I could play. I remember Coach (Bill) McCartney saying that the defense had to focus on me. He told me that he was looking forward to seeing me play the following season."

The 1980 season proved to be one of the most memorable of the 21 Bo Schembechler coached at Michigan. The Wolverines opened with a narrow win against Northwestern, but then lost on a last-second field goal at Notre Dame and again the following week to South Carolina and eventual Heisman Trophy winner George Rogers. After the loss to Notre Dame, Schembechler and his staff scrapped the Wolverines' option for a power running and passing attack. Michigan began to pound opponents with Ricks, Butch Woolfolk and Stanley Edwards running behind a vet-

LAWRENCE RICKS
Michigan letterman: 1979-1982

Position: Tailback **Number:** 46
Hometown: Barberton, Ohio

All-Big Ten, 1982
Career rushing: 541 carries, 2,751 yards, 24 TDs
Top game: 31 carries, 196 yards, 2 TDs at Purdue, 1982

eran line. The Wolverines ran the table to win the Big Ten championship and then defeated Washington to give Schembechler his first bowl victory. "That was probably the best trio of running backs at Michigan in a while," Ricks said. "We probably came closest to gaining 1,000 yards apiece."

Ricks ran for 850 yards, averaging 5.1 yards a carry. He had two big games that season, carrying 29 times for 184 yards and two touchdowns against California and 23 times for 123 yards and two touchdowns at Indiana. "That Indiana game stood out because we'd barely beaten them the season before," he said. "All three of us had a great game. It was a big game in terms of letting people know we were back."

Woolfolk, who was the MVP of the 1981 Rose Bowl, was the showcase back in 1981, his senior season. Ricks says he never complained about having to play a back-up role because he knew it was important for the team. He also was certain he would get his chance to be the showcase running back in 1982, his senior season. He led the Wolverines in rushing as a senior. He ran for 1,388 yards—averaging 5.2 yards a carry—and scored eight touchdowns. Michigan again won the Big Ten championship, but lost to UCLA in the 1983 Rose Bowl game.

Ricks delivered a strong performance in the season and Big Ten opener against Wisconsin, carrying 24 times for 153 yards and a touchdown. "That was an important game because we'd lost to them the season before," he said. He later had back-to-back games at Illinois and against Purdue in which he carried 31 times. He gained 177 yards against the Fighting Illini and 196 against the Boilermakers.

"My sophomore year, there was a lot of emotion because we started 1-2, but I felt there was more of a commitment on my part as a senior," he said. "Winning the Big Ten championship and going to the Rose Bowl—that's what you play for. Unfortunately, I think we had some problems with a lack of focus on the part of the younger guys when we went to the (1983) Rose Bowl. They didn't understand the opportunity and the expectation. They took it as more of a vacation than anything else." Ricks carried 23 times in that Rose Bowl game for 88 yards.

He was selected by Dallas in the eighth round of the 1983 NFL Draft, and he made it to the end of the Cowboys' training camp before being traded to Kansas City. He played two seasons with the Chiefs before injuries, including a detached retina, ended his career. He then returned to Michigan to complete his degree in computer engineering, with a major in computer science and a minor in electrical engineering.

A native of Schembechler's hometown of Barberton, Ohio, Ricks chose Michigan as much for academic as for athletic reasons. On his official visit to Ann Arbor, Schembechler introduced him to the dean of the School of Engineering. When Ricks and his father met later with Schembechler, the coach explained how he would be successful as a college student, not just as a football player. "Coach (Joe) Paterno was very similar at Penn State," he recalled. "He didn't sell football as much as he talked about how you fit into the school and his program."

Ricks worked for Goodyear Aerospace and IBM, which moved him to Lincoln, Nebraska, where he eventually met his wife, Cathy. He lived in Lincoln for 13 years, spending the last five working in state government. He moved to Columbus, Ohio, in 1998 to work for the state as a program analyst. He has spent the last four years as a contract employee in local database design, specializing in Medicare and Medicaid reimbursement.

Ricks and his wife have been married 15 years. The couple has three children: Christopher, 14; Tiffany, 10; and, Jessica, 2.

The 42-year-old Ricks admits that living in Columbus can be trying for a former Michigan football player. He constantly is challenged to defend his decision to go to Michigan, particularly for the education. "I can't get across to these people that Michigan is a great school," he said. "You get the impression they believe that every kid from Ohio has to go to Ohio State." He still gets excited about the Michigan-Ohio State rivalry, though he says he wishes fans would tone down their behavior. "They really need to establish a level of decency down here," he said. "The bad stuff takes away from the great games. The fans need to show the game the same respect the players do."

ERIC ROSEL

T he frustration in Eric Rosel's voice is easy to hear as he recites the litany of injuries that first sidetracked and eventually ended a promising college career.

Few athletes have been recruited to Michigan with more football credentials than Rosel, whose athleticism and versatility were such that he could have played just about anywhere. The expectation among coaches was that Rosel would succeed. The only question was at what position.

But it was not to be as anyone, particularly Rosel, expected. Almost from the moment he began to compete for a starting spot his redshirt freshman season (1998), he was dogged by injuries, many of them freakish in nature. "Every single frigging time things were going good, something would happen," he said. "Eventually, your position coach loses patience and turns to someone else. It was a frustrating deal."

Rosel, from Liberal, Kansas, wasn't planning to leave America's heartland to play football. Anyone in his family who had attended college had gone to the University of Kansas. His high school sweetheart went there, too, but she eventually transferred to Michigan. Rosel's recruiting horizons broadened dramatically after another Liberal product, tight end Jerame Tuman, headed to Ann Arbor and had great suc-

ERIC ROSEL
Michigan letterman: 1998-2001

Position: Tight end **Number:** 40
Hometown: Liberal, Kansas

Career statistics: 9 tackles; 2 catches for 20 yards

cess for the Wolverines. "There was a lot of pressure on me to stay in the Midlands," he said. "But on my very first visit to Michigan, as I was walking down the tunnel into the empty stadium, I could feel the history and the tradition of the program. That was my first recruiting visit, and it ruined it for the rest of them. Nothing else was the same."

Rosel sat out the 1997 national championship season as a redshirt, but he demonstrated so much potential on the defensive demonstration teams that he started the 1998 training camp battling senior Clint Copenhaver for the starting outside linebacker job. The competition didn't last long. Rosel broke both bones in his forearm during a practice drill and missed the next six weeks. He returned to the playing rotation in late October, but again he didn't remain healthy for long. Rosel was knocked to the ground during a home game against Indiana, and the force of the late hit tore the medial collateral ligament in his knee. He played in the regular-season finale at Hawaii, but he says he felt ridiculous because he was so out of sync.

Michigan defensive coaches began to question Rosel's toughness and durability, so he got fewer opportunities to prove himself, though he did play a lot on special teams. Sensing his growing frustration, tight ends coach Mike DeBord, who had recruited Rosel out of Kansas, asked him to switch to that position. Rosel agreed, eager for a fresh start.

Again, injuries took their toll. Back in Liberal for a visit the summer before his fifth season, Rosel underwent an appendectomy. Doctors also discovered a hernia that Rosel had caused the previous summer while lifting weights. Two days after his first surgery, doctors repaired the hernia. The two operations shut down his conditioning program for the entire summer. Once again, Rosel bounced back, determined to play injury free for at least one season, but it was not to be.

In addition to the other injuries, Rosel suffered five concussions during his Michigan career. The last occurred during a 20-0 win at Penn State in 2001. As he followed through on a fake from his H-back position, he was smacked under the chin by a defender. "I was never right for two months after that deal," he said. "I had to lay off a month, so I could have come back for the Ohio State game or maybe for the bowl game, but doctors told me if I was hit again bad, it could cause brain damage. I had ambitions beyond football, so I did not want to risk it. Coach (Lloyd) Carr agreed with the decision. But it was a tough day when I had to walk away from football."

Rosel had enrolled at Michigan determined to become a doctor, but he quickly realized after he had opportunities to follow doctors around that his career choice was not the right one. After graduating with a degree in bio-psychology and cognitive sciences, he decided to go into the family business.

His grandfather started The Rosel Company, an oil field service company, in 1959 in Perryton, Texas, and eventually expanded the business into Oklahoma and Kansas. Rosel and his father, who had tried to steer his son into a different career because of the volatility of the oil business, are the only two family members still connected with the company. Rosel works in sales and marketing for the company out of Oklahoma City, covering all of that state, northern Texas and southern Kansas. He has been a licensed pilot since he was 17, and he flies his single-engine Cessna 182RG on most business trips. "To go into that business without family connections, I would have needed a degree in petroleum engineering or geology," he said. "But I learned by doing. I started learning the grunt aspects of the job when I was three years old."

Rosel married Kaely, whom he'd known since the seventh grade, after both graduated from Michigan in 2002. The couple has one son, Kelly, born earlier this year.

Though Rosel tries to remain philosophical about the injuries and the toll they took, there are days when his frustration boils over. "The thing is, you fight so hard all those years—I remember waking up at 5:30 in the morning during the summer to run the golf course—and for an injury to take you out is so horrible," he said. "You sacrifice everything for this sport, and to not be able to finish is so hard. I'm the kind of person who wants to finish everything I start. This just feels incomplete. It's hard to reach a comfort inside myself."

Where Have You Gone?

DOUG SKENE

Doug Skene is proud of his class—so proud, in fact, that he believes it stacks up against any class of any generation to play at Michigan in terms of its overall quality.

It's a bold assertion, to be sure, but Skene believes he has plenty of evidence. Including its first season, when Skene and most of his classmates redshirted, the class helped Michigan win four outright Big Ten championships and a share of a fifth. It would participate in four Rose Bowls, produce a Heisman Trophy winner (Desmond Howard) and three All-Americans, and send seven players to the National Football League.

"I got into it once with Mike Leoni about my class and his class, but I have always said 'arguably,'" Skene said. "How do you really gauge it? You can look at it a lot of ways. I have a picture of us from media day our senior year in my office, and to my recollection, we were part of the only stretch when Michigan won five Big Ten titles in a row. We were on every one of those championship teams. I'm one of 14 guys who has five rings."

Skene is equally as passionate about the fifth-year senior-dominated offensive line that led Michigan to a 9-0-3 record in 1992 and a 38-31 win against Washington in the 1993 Rose Bowl. With Skene and

Photo courtesy of Bob Kalmbach, University of Michigan

DOUG SKENE
Michigan letterman: 1989-1992

Position: Guard **Number:** 72
Hometown: Fairview, Texas

All-Big Ten, 1992

classmates Steve Everett, Joe Cocozzo and Rob Doherty opening gaping holes in the Huskies' defense, sophomore tailback Tyrone Wheatley exploded for 235 yards and three touchdowns, including one on an 88-yard scamper that still stands as the longest run in Rose Bowl history. During the past decade, that group has been the standard to which all Michigan offensive linemen have held themselves.

"When you get to be a fifth-year senior and you've been running the same offense for four years, you can pick up your blocking assignments in your sleep," he said. "That allows guys to go out and have fun and beat the snot out of people. Your assignments are almost secondary in your head. You would go up to the line, and the guy (with no one to block) would look for someone to tee off on. We'd go out there looking to demoralize people. The ball would be snapped, and you'd be looking to mess with someone."

Skene remembers Everett doing just that to Washington defensive lineman DeMarco Farr in the '93 Rose Bowl game. Everett so physically beat up on and verbally abused him that by the fourth quarter Farr could not look Everett in the eye. "Everett had ridden him so hard that even his own teammates were laughing at him," Skene recalled. "And the guy went on to have a pretty good pro career."

Because offensive linemen typically toil in anonymity, Skene says Michigan linemen would go out of their way during games to get a little animated so that they would have a good laugh the following day while watching film. "The ball would be snapped, and we'd be looking to mess around with someone," he said. "We'd go out of our way to make a dramatic pancake block. Everett would tee someone up, and I'd nail him in the side of the head. We did that to freshmen in practice all the time, too."

That was a rite of passage in Michigan football that Skene understood well. He'd been smacked around plenty during his freshman season by veterans such as Mark Messner and J.J. Grant, and he'd learned from the experience. Once during Michigan State week his freshman season, when he played Spartans star Tony Mandarich on the demonstration team, an assistant coach told him to take a run at middle guard Mike Teeter to spice up the practice a bit. Skene did as he was instructed, and in the ensuing fight, Teeter picked him up and body-slammed him to the ground. Skene weighed 290 pounds.

Skene had wanted to play football for Michigan as long as he could remember. He lived in Hartland, Michigan, just north of Ann Arbor, until his family moved to Texas when he was 10. His friends in Fairview, Texas, dreamed of playing in the Southwest Conference. Not Skene.

During his freshman year he wrote to Michigan coach Bo Schembechler to inform him of his interest in playing for the Wolverines. He got a form letter back from Michigan assistant Cam Cameron, who recruited the state of Texas. Skene had the same letter exchange with Cameron his sophomore year.

The situation changed dramatically after his junior season, when Skene was named the defensive linemen of the year in his conference. Suddenly, every big school in the country had an interest in him. The summer before his senior year, while he and his family visited friends in Michigan, he was invited to attend the Wolverines' summer camp. Texas high school rules prohibited players from participating in such camps, so he watched from the sideline. Later that day he and his parents met with Schembechler, who offered Skene a scholarship. He accepted immediately. "How many thousands of kids grow up dreaming about playing for Michigan?" he said. "I was that same kid, but I had a chance."

He also got a chance to play in the NFL. Philadelphia selected him in the eighth round of the 1993 Draft, but he lasted only half a season with the Eagles before they cut him from their practice squad. He played briefly on New Orleans' practice squad before New England coach Bill Parcells offered him a spot on the Patriots' active roster. He earned a starting spot his second year with the team, but halfway through the season, he suffered a serious knee injury. After intense rehabilitation, he tried to make a comeback with the Patriots in 1995, but he was cut. Green Bay offered him a contract for the 1996 season, so he moved back to Ann Arbor to train. He asked Michigan head trainer Paul Schmidt to take a look at his knee one day. Schmidt told him that if he continued to play football, he would accelerate problems, such as arthritis, that were certain to occur later in life. "I didn't want to be the guy who couldn't walk because he'd hung on too long," he said. "It was time to take a new road."

Skene moved to East Tawas, Michigan, and went to work as a salesman for Coca-Cola Enterprises in Bay City. He managed route drivers and the merchandising staff. He has worked the past five years as a manufacturer's representative for General Cigar Company. His territory is the state of Michigan and Toledo, Ohio.

He is back living in the Hartland area. He and his wife, Tracy, celebrated their 10th anniversary this year. They have two children, Nathan, 6, and Madelin, 3, and they were expecting a third in June.

Skene admits that at times he is amazed at the success he and his classmates enjoyed at Michigan, particularly when he remembers how

big a deal it was for Michigan fans last fall when the Wolverines quali-
fied to play in the Rose Bowl for the first time since the 1997 season.

"I did that four times in my career," he said. "Have things changed
that much, or were our teams that good? I think it's a combination of
both. College football has changed, no doubt, but we had some good
players. Michigan still does. The next guy will step in, and Michigan will
be there for the Big Ten championship at the end of the season. There's
always the next guy."

Where Have You Gone?

TOM SLADE

Considering Tom Slade's background, it isn't surprising that games against Michigan State figure so prominently in his Michigan career.

Anyone in his family who had gone to college had attended MSU, and his uncle had played quarterback for the Spartans. MSU coaches were the first to recruit him, while he was a sophomore at Saginaw (Michigan) High School. "I came within an eyelash of going to Michigan State," Slade said.

Instead, he went to Michigan. "It was a matter of a winged helmet and a great school," he said. "That was where I wanted to go, but (Michigan coaches) never asked me, so I assumed they didn't want me. Michigan didn't say a word to me until just before the (1969) Ohio State game. That was my first contact with Michigan." The wait didn't bother Slade, who immediately accepted when Coach Bo Schembechler offered him a scholarship in early December. "It was a very difficult recruiting thing for Bo," Slade said with a grin.

Slade, now 52, started only in 1971 at quarterback, but it was a season he and his teammates will savor for a lifetime. The Wolverines finished the regular season 11-0, becoming the first Michigan team to do so since 1948. The Wolverines eventually lost a heartbreaker to Stanford

TOM SLADE
Michigan letterman: 1971-1973

Position: Quarterback **Number:** 17
Hometown: Saginaw, Michigan

Career passing: 27 of 64 for 364 yards, 2 TDs, 4 interceptions
Career rushing: 89 carries, 270 yards, 3 TDs
Top game: 11 carries, 48 yards, 1 TD at Michigan State, 1971

in the Rose Bowl, but they still take pride in being the only Schembechler-coached team to win all 11 games during the regular season.

With Don Moorhead graduated, the 1971 quarterback competition pitted Slade against Kevin Casey and Larry Cipa. Casey, who Slade said was the best athlete of the three, eventually emerged as No. 1 and started the first four games. But Casey began to lose playing time to Slade following a close win against Northwestern in the season opener. Casey played three quarters and Slade played one against Virginia, the two split time equally against Tulane, and Slade played three quarters to Casey's one against Navy.

The Tuesday of the following week—with the Michigan State game looming—Schembechler told Slade to work with the first offense, and he did all week. "Nobody ever told me I would start," he said. "I thought maybe … I didn't know what to think. I just did it. By Thursday, I'm thinking maybe I'm going to play. I told my folks: I might start this thing. But Bo never called me in his office, never sat me down, and never told me they were going to make a change and that I was going to start. Maybe that was good because it kept me on the cutting edge all week. I'm thinking maybe I'm there, but I didn't want to screw it up. I thought maybe one big mistake in practice might knock me off that perch."

With Slade running the offense, the Wolverines survived a miserable, rainy afternoon in East Lansing to post a 24-13 win. The game was televised nationally, which at that time was a huge deal. Slade scored the touchdown that sealed the win on a down-the-line option to the right heading into the north end zone at Spartan Stadium. "I nosed a guy up at the 5-yard line, spun around him and got into the end zone," he said.

The Wolverines drove to within a yard of the same end zone with just seconds remaining in the game. Just when it appeared time would expire, a Michigan player called a timeout. After Slade handed off the ball on the final play, he carried through his fake around the right end and continued up the tunnel and into the Michigan locker room, where he collapsed on a pile of mats. "I was totally wiped out," he said. "I can honestly say in my life, I was never as exhausted mentally and physically as I was at that moment."

Slade suffered a hip injury early in the season finale against Ohio State, and he said he was so gimpy that he could not get down the line on the option or to block on the sweep. At halftime, Slade told coaches he was too hurt to continue. "I basically pulled myself, which was probably the end of my career, but it was stupid to play me," he said. Cipa took over and completed a long pass to Bo Rather that set up the winning touchdown run by Billy Taylor. Fullback Fritz Seyferth threw a crushing block on Taylor's run, but Slade insists that Cipa was the key to the play's success. "He ended up blocking the guy he was supposed to option," Slade said. "The guy wouldn't be optioned, so Cipa pitched it anyway to Taylor and then blocked the guy. That play never happens without Cipa. I can tell you, as hurt as I was, I would never have been able to get that guy."

Michigan's bid for a perfect season ended with a 13-12 loss to Stanford in the Rose Bowl, but Slade says the Wolverines were in trouble the minute their plane touched down in southern California two weeks earlier. Their practice field at a junior college was underwater—groundskeepers supposedly had forgotten to turn off some sprinklers—and conditions only got worse. The next day, it began to rain and never stopped. "The only guy going to survive this thing is Noah," Slade said. The Wolverines were forced to work out indoors and tried to stay in shape by running laps around the hotel grounds. Finally, a disgusted Schembechler put the team on a plane to Bakersfield, California, where the team trained for two days in cold, but dry conditions. By the time the team returned to Los Angeles, many of the players were sick.

"It actually got nice for the game, but the field had no grass on it," Slade said. "It was all paint. It was one of the ugliest Rose Bowl fields you ever saw. Then, we get in a dogfight with Stanford, and it turns out they have some great players. It was an era where you didn't see those teams like you do now. It was like they were from the moon. They played us nose to nose, and we weren't ready or in shape. We were everything but ready, but we still hammered it out with them."

It also was Slade's last game at quarterback. The following spring, he was fifth on the depth chart behind starter Dennis Franklin. He did hold for extra-point and field-goal attempts. By his senior season, however, he'd even lost that job. Then, in early October, Slade was stunned to learn that he was no longer on the travel roster. "Guess where we were going? Michigan State," he said.

Slade enrolled in Michigan's School of Dentistry in 1974—he later learned that a one-sentence letter of recommendation from Schembechler clinched his admission—and he finished in 1978. After working for other dentists in Fenton and South Lyon for three years, Slade purchased a practice in Ypsilanti, where he has worked since.

Slade, the father of two teenaged sons, has tried to remain active in athletics. He was a Division I-A college basketball referee for 26 years, and he continues to serve as an evaluator of officials for the Mid-American Conference. He has worked off and on the past two decades as a radio commentator for both Michigan and Eastern Michigan football games. He last worked with Tom Hemingway on WUOM broadcasts of Michigan football until the conclusion of the 2000 season.

Slade says time has helped to put into perspective what he and his teammates accomplished during that memorable 1971 season. "We win those 11 games and don't think much of it then," he said. "We just did what we were supposed to do. Hells bells, it took 26 years for some other (Michigan) team to do it. Now you really understand how big it was what you did."

PAUL STAROBA

Paul Staroba didn't hesitate when a Flint television sportscaster asked him if he believed he had a future in college football. He intended to play football in the Big Ten, he answered. Mark Abbott, his backfield mate on the unbeaten Flint St. Matthew High School varsity football team, couldn't believe what he was hearing. "He told me people would think I was nuts," Staroba recalled.

But Staroba believed he belonged in the Big Ten. His high school coach had taken him the previous season to Michigan's spring intrasquad scrimmage game. As the two stood along the sidelines in Michigan Stadium, the coach compared Staroba to some of the Michigan players, pointing out that he was as big as many of them and faster than some. "When you're a kid, those college players seem like gods to you," he said. "The coach played a lot with my mind. The things he was telling me made those players seem more human."

Staroba admits his notion of playing in the Big Ten revolved, at least initially, around playing at Michigan State. In the mid-1960s, the Spartans were the scourge of the conference, and many talented players from the Flint area gravitated to East Lansing. Staroba wanted to go there, too, but MSU coaches weren't interested in a player from a tiny Class D Catholic school. As it turned out, Staroba had an "in" at

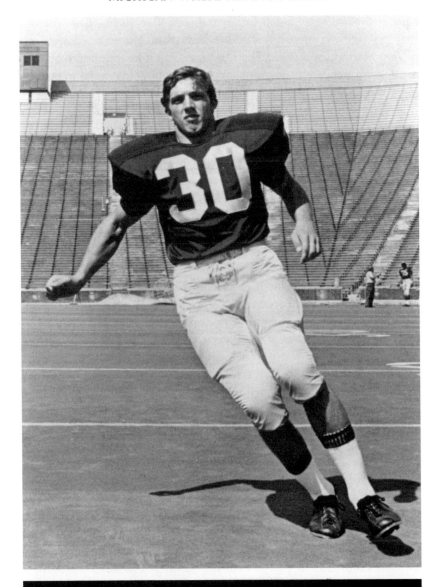

PAUL STAROBA
Michigan letterman: 1968-1970

Position: Split end **Number:** 30
Hometown: Flint, Michigan

All-Big Ten, 1970
Career receiving: 58 catches, 818 yards, 4 TDs
Top game: 6 catches, 178 yards, 1 TD at Wisconsin, 1970

Michigan—his future father-in-law and boss, Tom Ryan, who took him to games and the annual post-season bust. Ryan also was a close friend of Tom Harmon and Forest Evashevski, and after he introduced Staroba to those former Michigan greats, Staroba was only interested in becoming a Wolverine.

That almost didn't happen, however. More interested in athletics than academics in high school, Staroba did not qualify academically to play in the freshman program at Michigan. Taking a job as a sheet metal worker the summer after he graduated from high school, he earned enough to pay his first year's tuition at Michigan. Though Staroba did not play or practice with the Wolverines his freshman year, Coach Bump Elliott offered him a scholarship based on Ryan's recommendation.

"Coming to Michigan was the best thing that ever happened to me," he said. "I was very fortunate that I had some doors opened to me, but I was smart enough to walk through them."

Staroba was a running back in high school, but he moved to wide receiver in college. He played that position in 1968, Elliott's final season, catching 11 passes for 158 yards and two touchdowns. Staroba tried to play wingback in 1969 for first-year coach Bo Schembechler, but the position switch didn't work well. Staroba sprained both his thumbs, which made catching the ball difficult. To make matters worse, Staroba admits, he didn't get along well with his new coach. "Bo was not happy and I had a bad attitude, so I was getting a lot of pine time," said Staroba, who caught passes in just three games that season. "Pretty soon I realized that I had better get my act together or I would be spending my senior year on the bench, too. I wasn't on the same page as the coach, and I figured I'd better get there."

With an improved attitude, Staroba reported to camp his senior season in great shape, and he earned a starting job as a wide receiver. Against Michigan State, he caught six passes for 80 yards in a 34-20 victory that avenged the Wolverines' only Big Ten loss the previous season. Two weekends later against Wisconsin, he caught six more passes for a career-high 178 yards and a touchdown. He says his former teammates will never let him forget the touchdown he did not score in that game. Catching a throwback pass from his best friend Don Moorhead, Staroba rumbled to the Wisconsin 3-yard line before being tackled. "I tell people that when I got to the 5, I tried to dive in and only got to the 3," he said. "I never wanted to admit I got caught from behind."

Staroba also punted his senior season, and did it well enough to end up in the school record book. He finished that season with 2,240 yards, which ranks eighth all-time. He punted for 401 yards in a game against

Arizona. It is the fourth best single-game total in school history. He finished fourth in the nation with a 41.5 yard average. Staroba said he learned to punt by kicking the ball to his father over the roof of his house. His mother stopped the practice after one of his punts knocked the television attenna loose.

Staroba also might have been remembered for delivering one of the longest punts in school history. He hit a 76-yarder out of the end zone at Ohio State in his final game but it was nullified by a penalty. He did score the Wolverines' only touchdown in that game on a short pass from Moorhead. He still has a newspaper photo of his celebration in the end zone with Moorhead, Reggie McKenzie and Dan Dierdorf. The Wolverines lost, 20-9. "What people don't remember about that Michigan-Ohio State game is that both teams were undefeated," he said.

Selected by Cleveland in the third round of the 1971 NFL Draft, Staroba played two seasons with the Browns before being traded to Washington, where he was cut just before the season opener. Green Bay picked him up, and he punted in the final two games of the season. He had his most memorable pro moment in the finale against Chicago. After fielding a low snap off the turf and seeing nothing but black jerseys coming at him, he faked the punt and scrambled for a first down. Having blocked one of Staroba's earlier punts, the Bears rushers jumped when he faked the kick, and he was able to elude them.

With his pro career finished, Staroba went to work for his father-in-law's Anheuser-Busch beer distributorship in Flint. He is still the general manager of the company. He and his wife, Wendy, were married 30 years and are now divorced. He has five daughters—Jennifer, Stephanie, Aimee, Sarah and Samantha—whose ages range from 29 to 15. He lives in Grand Blanc, Michigan.

Staroba likes to point out that he wasn't the only player from his St. Matthew football team to make a contribution to Michigan. His backfield mate, Mike Abbott's son, Jim, would eventually become one of the finest pitchers in the history of the baseball program.

Where Have You Gone?

JAKE SWEENEY

No player did more to convince current Michigan head coach Lloyd Carr of the importance of having a good long snapper than Jake Sweeney.

In 1979, the season before Carr joined Bo Schembechler's staff and Sweeney came to Michigan from Alma High School, the Wolverines lost their final two games (and, as a result, the Big Ten championship) because of blocked punts that were returned for touchdowns. Schembechler made it clear from the first day of spring practice that there would be a renewed emphasis on protecting the punter. For the next four seasons, protection for Michigan's punters and kickers would start with Sweeney's snaps.

"Larry Sweeney was maybe the best long snapper I've ever seen," Carr said in 2002. "In those four years, we never had a kick blocked. Every ball was perfect. And we won some championships." Larry? More about that later.

Carr's right about the championships—the Wolverines earned Big Ten titles in 1980 and 1982 and won the 1981 Rose Bowl—but his memory is a tad faulty in terms of Sweeney's perfection. Turns out, Sweeney made two mistakes. That's still a amazing total, considering he

JAKE SWEENEY
Michigan letterman: 1980-1983

Position: Center **Number:** 55
Hometown: Alma, Michigan

made 706 snaps for punts, extra points and field goals in 48 consecutive career games.

While Carr has forgotten those mistakes with the passing of two decades, Sweeney has not. In fact, when he's asked to recount the highlights of his career, he recalls the two that went bad. "A moment that stands out?" he said, mulling over the question. "I guess that depends on how you look at it."

Some student fan at Michigan Stadium deserves an assist on his first "bad" snap during the 1981 game against Notre Dame. Back then, the first time in a game the Wolverines would score a touchdown in the north end zone, students would hurl rolls of toilet paper onto the field. After the Wolverines' second touchdown in a 25-7 win against the Irish, a roll landed right in front of holder B.J. Dickey as he prepared to take the extra-point snap from Sweeney. Dickey reached down and brushed it aside. Peering back between his legs, Sweeney mistook Dickey's motion for the hand signal Michigan used to initiate extra-point and field-goal attempts. "I saw that, and I figured he was ready," Sweeney said. "I used to snap blind, because I knew where I was going. So I fired it."

As Dickey turned to make certain kicker Ali Haji-Sheikh was ready, Sweeney's snap hit him right in the ear hole of his helmet. The snap was perfect—Dickey's helmet was where his hands would have been—but the ball bounced high into the air and Haji-Sheikh was swarmed under by tacklers when he grabbed the ball. Both Sweeny and Dickey understood the significance of a lost extra point—Michigan had lost by two points to Notre Dame the previous season on a last-second field goal—so neither was eager to return to the Michigan sideline to face Schembechler. "B.J. and I were both pointing fingers at each other," Sweeney said. Both players could laugh about the goof later that week, because it was featured on Johnny Carson's *Tonight Show* as a football blooper.

The other "bad" snap resulted in a blocked punt during a 58-10 Michigan win at Minnesota in Sweeney's senior season. The Gophers lined up Norrice Wilson, the Big Ten's biggest player, over Sweeney, who was playing with an injured hamstring. What Sweeney and other blockers didn't realize is that Minnesota hid a small defensive back behind Wilson who rushed in unimpeded after the ball was snapped and blocked Don Bracken's punt. Sweeney was initially blamed for the block because his snap was lower than usual to Bracken, who liked to get the ball just above the knee. "But it was a blocking breakdown," Sweeney said. "It could have been a perfect snap, and the punt still would have been blocked."

Sweeney's father and grandfather both played football at Central Michigan, but he'd always hoped to follow in the footsteps of his father, who'd played quarterback. Instead, he wound up at his grandfather's position—center. Sweeney grew up hanging around football practices at Alma College, where his father was an assistant coach. He was in the fifth grade when Alma's center showed him how to long snap. By the time Sweeney began playing football in the eighth grade, he could long snap as well as any player on the college team.

"That's when my dad talked me into not being a quarterback," he said. "I just jumped into the center spot, and I was there my whole career. But my dad believed that if you were going to be a center, you had to do everything. That was your job: You touched the ball on every offensive play."

Sweeney's father encouraged his son's all-around excellence by rewarding him for good grades and keeping his football skills in shape. Each morning in the gym balcony, Sweeney took 100 snaps, half going the distance to a punter and the other half to a holder on place-kicks. By the time he was a senior, he could deliver the ball to the punter with the laces on the ball pointing straight up in less than seven-tenths of a second. Once while he was being recruited, two Michigan State assistants clocked him with a stopwatch because they didn't believe he could get the ball back that quickly.

Before committing to Michigan, Sweeney asked Schembechler whether he could play as a freshman if he proved to be the team's best long snapper. Schembechler responded: "If you can snap that ball as good as you say you can, I'll play you from the day you walk in here."

Sweeney never played in the NFL—because of reduced roster sizes, few teams then carried a specialist such as a long snapper—but Bracken later told him that he was better than any pro long snapper with whom he'd worked.

Not long after he'd graduated from Michigan, Sweeney met an old friend from Alma who worked for the Bureau of Alcohol, Tobacco and Firearms. She encouraged him to apply for a job with the Federal Bureau of Investigation. He interviewed, but was told there were no jobs available. Instead, he joined the United States Border Patrol.

"It is the Marine Corps of federal law enforcement," he said. "They put you through the hardest training there is—21 weeks in south Georgia—teach you to speak Spanish and then send you to a third-world border town. I thought: 'Twenty-one weeks in south Georgia can't be tougher than four years with Bo Schembechler.'"

After three years in Douglas, Arizona, Sweeney worked for 10 years as a physical training instructor at the U.S. Border Patrol Academy. He took an early retirement because "at age 33, you realize that your ego can no longer sustain your body." After working briefly as a representative for a company that manufactured police batons, he became president of PDS Lighting, his own wholesale distribution company for LED lighting.

He and his wife, Dawn, also a Michigan alum, have been married since 1987. The couple has two children, Jake and Allie. Dawn is a national sales director for Mary Kay Cosmetics. "That explains the lifestyle I have as an ex-civil servant who hawks flashlights for a living," Sweeney said.

Coaches such as Carr call Sweeney by his given name, Larry, but his former teammates know him by his nickname, Jake. Long-time Michigan equipment manager Jon Falk began calling him that almost from the minute he reported to training camp as a freshman. Falk, who hails from southern Ohio, picked it because Sweeney's last name reminded him of a Cincinnati automobile dealer named Jake Sweeney. "A lot of guys don't know my real name is Larry," Sweeney said.

BILLY TAYLOR

Any time Billy Taylor needs a jolt of enthusiasm these days, he pops in a videotape that recounts the "10-Year War" between Bo Schembechler's Michigan and Woody Hayes's Ohio State teams. Taylor, who played on the first three of those Michigan teams, particularly enjoys watching Michigan's 10-7 win against the Buckeyes at Michigan Stadium in 1971. Not surprisingly, his favorite moment is his 21-yard touchdown run with 2:07 remaining that clinched the victory.

That run—recalled by many Michigan football fans because of Bob Ufer's screaming "Touchdown, Billy Taylor!" radio call—stood as Taylor's legacy for more than three decades, during which he served time in prison for his part in an armed robbery and eventually sank into the hellish oblivion of alcohol and drug addiction. He drifted so far from former teammates and coaches that many of them stopped wondering what had happened to him, preferring instead to remember the player and friend they once knew.

As much as he still loves to reminisce about his Michigan career and the famous run that punctuated it with an exclamation point, Taylor would rather be remembered these days for the walk he took a little more than a year ago. On May 17, 2003, Taylor stepped onto the stage in a University of Nevada-Las Vegas auditorium to accept a doctorate in edu-

BILLY TAYLOR
Michigan letterman: 1969-1971

Position: Tailback **Number:** 42
Hometown: Barberton, Ohio

All-American, 1971
Career rushing: 587 carries, 3,072 yards, 30 TDs
Top game: 21 carries, 225 yards, 2 TDs at Iowa, 1969

cation leadership. When he returned to Michigan Stadium that fall for the 100th Michigan-Ohio State game, he came back as "Dr." Billy Taylor.

"Bo Schembechler had a never-give-up attitude. That was his philosophy, and it is my philosophy," Taylor said. "If you set goals and work hard enough, you can achieve success. I believe in our old team motto, that those who stay will be champions. I am still a champion in my own mind, especially when I walked across that stage and heard them announce 'Dr. William Taylor.' That was the greatest personal achievement in my life. That was my best moment since I scored that touchdown against Ohio State."

He now works at the 35,000-student Community College of Southern Nevada. He was able to use the master's degree he'd earned from Michigan while in prison to begin a career as a professor of English, and he still teaches some classes. His official title at the school now is National Junior College Athletic Association compliance officer and student advisor. He also serves as interim director of student retention, managing a 31-person staff that helps wavering students remain in school. It is a job, he believes, for which his life experiences have prepared him well.

Taylor admits that his Michigan football career—he finished with 3,072 career rushing yards, was a three-time All-Big Ten performer and was voted the team's most valuable player following his senior season—now often seems as if it occurred in another lifetime, separated from the present by years of hopelessness and despair.

He's battled depression since his mother, Mariah Marie Taylor, died unexpectedly three days after Michigan lost to Stanford in the 1972 Rose Bowl, and it only got worse in the months that followed after his girlfriend was stabbed to death in Detroit and his favorite uncle murdered his aunt and then killed himself. He blames those deaths, particularly his mother's, for causing him to lose interest in football and steadily increase a drinking problem that eventually cost him his marriage.

Taylor was drafted by Atlanta in the '72 NFL Draft, but he never was comfortable with Falcons head coach Norm Van Brocklin. Not long after he spoke up about what he believed was unfair criticism of the team's black players, he was cut. After bouncing briefly around the league, he finished the season with the Calgary Stampeders of the Canadian Football League. He attempted an NFL comeback the following season with the Philadelphia Eagles, but a knee injury finished his career.

Returning to his hometown of Barberton, Ohio, Taylor coped with his depression by drinking and partying. After a night of heavy drinking, he gave an acquaintance a ride, not knowing the man had just committed an armed robbery. Taylor was arrested and served 2 1/2 years in the federal penitentiary in Milan, Michigan. He did not waste the time. Schembechler and Dr. Bill Donovan, the dean of Michigan's graduate school of education, set up a work-study program that enabled Taylor to earn a master's degree in education. A straight-A student, Taylor became the first inmate to earn a graduate degree while serving federal time.

Taylor was married in 1978. At the time, he was working for General Motors as a second-shift maintenance supervisor. His depression came to a head in the early 1980s when he refused to transfer to work in a southern state after GM ended operations at the plant in which he was working. He went on unemployment and began to drink even more heavily than before. His marriage and his life fell apart. "I experienced all of the bad things that go along with negative habits," he said. "I am just blessed to be alive. I thank God each day for my second life."

His "second life" began August 17, 1997, when he heard a voice telling him to "come forth" and to "talk to the lady in the red van" about a job. That woman was Sheryl Carson, the owner and founder of "Family Ties," a company that runs adult foster care homes on Detroit's east side. She put Taylor to work doing yard chores. It was the opportunity he needed, a chance to get out of the streets. He eventually became Carson's right-hand man, and the two forged such a tight relationship that he calls her "Sis."

In 1998, Carson took her employees on a Western vacation that included a stop in Las Vegas. Taylor read in the local newspaper that the city was desperate for high school and junior college teachers. After returning to Detroit, Taylor told Carson he'd always wanted to finish the doctorate he'd started at Michigan, and he thought he could do that and get a teaching job in Nevada. He loaded up his 1988 Pontiac Bonneville, a car he called "Black Beauty," and headed west.

The Community College of Southern Nevada hired him as an English professor, and he taught composition classes at night while attending his doctoral classes at Nevada-Las Vegas. Eventually, he became involved with the community college's athletic programs. The team colors are maize and blue. "That alone let me know I was in the right place," he said.

Taylor has three children, and he said he has a good relationship with each of them. His sons, William Taylor III and Alden James Butch

Taylor, both attend college in the state of Michigan. His teenage daughter, Mariah Marie Taylor, lives in Detroit with her mother.

Taylor has returned to Ann Arbor the past seven years to attend reunions of the 1969 and 1971 Michigan teams, and he was particularly pleased to be part of the gauntlet of former players who greeted the Wolverines when they took the field to play Ohio State in 2003. That was the first time in years many ex-Wolverines had seen Taylor, and they were both stunned and pleased to see the change in him.

"I'm 55, but I feel like I'm going on 18," he said. "I have the top degree offered anywhere, and I am very proud of that. But I know that if I had not had that work ethic from Michigan, I would never have completed it."

Where Have You Gone?

MICHAEL TAYLOR

As former Michigan quarterback Michael Taylor reflects on and tries to make peace with his college football career, he remains convinced it should have been different.

He believes he would have started sooner had coaches relied less on favoritism and judged competition in practice and performance in games more fairly—perceived slights that prompted him to clash often with his position coach. He also endured a series of injuries during his career, including a serious upper-arm injury in his fifth season (1989) that caused him to miss four games. He remains angry about that injury, in particular, because he believes coaches and team doctors never were honest with him about the severity of the damage and because he says Michigan officials refused to help him pay for private treatment for the injury once his playing career was finished.

"I have learned to deal with it," Taylor said of his disappointment regarding his career. "I love my university, and I always will. Anyone who knows me knows how I feel about Michigan. But I went through more things to get out on the football field than any man should have to go through, and that's not right. And I'm not the only one who went through it."

Photo courtesy of Bob Kalmbach, University of Michigan

MICHAEL TAYLOR
Michigan letterman: 1987-1989

Position: Quarterback **Number:** 9
Hometown: Lincoln Heights, Ohio

Career passing: 163 of 275 for 2,194 yards, 17 TDs, 7 interceptions
Career rushing: 182 carries, 610 yards, 9 TDs
Top game: 12-of-16 passing for 231 yards, 4 TDs

Taylor had grand dreams for college, and he believed Michigan coaches shared them. From the moment Michigan began to recruit Taylor out of Cincinnati Princeton High School in 1984, Coach Bo Schembechler made it clear that no prospect was more important. In fact, Taylor says, Schembechler was so determined to bring him to Ann Arbor that he once told him he didn't trust anyone else on the staff to recruit him. "I remember Bo called me from the locker room after they were embarrassed at Iowa, and he asked me if I had watched the game," Taylor said. "Then he said: 'Now you know why I need you.'"

Despite such appeals, Taylor wasn't the only quarterback Michigan recruited that year. The Wolverines also landed Demetrious Brown, who three seasons later would compete with Taylor for the starting position. Taylor said competition didn't scare him because he had confidence in his abilities. "I love Demetrious," he said. "I figured out after my freshman season that it wasn't about me and him being enemies. Both of us pushed each other."

Heading into the 1987 season, the two third-year players were locked in a tight race to replace the departed Jim Harbaugh, but Taylor says that even as assistant coach Gary Moeller assured him that the competition was far from over and that he perceived no difference between the two quarterbacks, Brown began to practice more with the first offense and eventually was named the starter. Taylor says he was told before several games that he would get significant playing time, but he never left the bench. His frustration mounted in early October as he watched Brown throw seven interceptions in a 17-11 loss at Michigan State.

After Brown injured his thumb in a loss at Indiana, Taylor finally got his first start against Northwestern. He thought he made the most of his opportunity, breaking off four runs of more than 30 yards, including one for 65 yards and a touchdown. Once Brown was cleared to return to action, however, Taylor was back on the bench.

Taylor said he and Moeller argued regularly, and he admits it probably hurt his chances of playing more often. "If you stand up for yourself, you're labeled as a kid with an attitude problem," he said. So Taylor tried to fight back. "The week of the Ohio State game, I did something I had never done before: I didn't care what I did out there in practice," he said. "At some point I had had enough. I thought: 'If they are not going to play me, why should I bust my butt? Why go through the hassle if you're not going to play because someone doesn't like you?' I figured I wasn't going to play, so I threw interceptions on purpose."

Ironically, Taylor had to relieve the injured Brown during the game, which the Buckeyes rallied to win, 23-20.

After academic issues sidelined Brown for a time in 1988, Taylor started nine games to help lead the Wolverines back to the Rose Bowl. He would have started in the Rose Bowl, but he broke his collarbone during practice the week before the game.

With Brown gone in 1989, Taylor had the starting job to himself, but he again had to fight through injuries. During a passing drill the week before the opener against Notre Dame, he felt something pop in his shoulder. He later learned that he'd torn the bicep and tricep tendon in his rotator cuff. Despite soreness, he played against Notre Dame until a tackler hit him the back—a collision that cracked three vertebrae. He was forced to sit for three games while redshirt freshman Elvis Grbac played, but the time off helped to strengthen his arm. When he returned, he was stunned to learn that he had to win his job back from Grbac. He did, and he led the Wolverines back to the Rose Bowl.

Taylor played what he considers to be the best game of his career that season at Minnesota. Possibly because the game was played indoors at the Metrodome, his arm felt great, and he threw four touchdown passes in a 45-15 victory. A fifth touchdown pass was nullified by a penalty. But the following week in practice, with the Ohio State game looming, his arm strength progressively diminished. Still, Taylor was determined to gut it out, and he helped the Wolverines pull out a 28-18 win. The injury flared up the week before the Rose Bowl, and again Taylor played through it. The game against Southern Cal eventually turned in the fourth quarter when a holding penalty nullified a successful faked punt by Michigan, and the Wolverines lost 17-10.

With his career concluded, Taylor sought the help of his former high school physician regarding his arm injury, but he says Michigan athletic officials told him they would not pay for any surgery unless it was performed by a team doctor. Taylor was incensed. "To go through what I did and have them tell you they are under no obligation to fix my shoulder, that's hard to swallow," he said. "That's the worst moment of my Michigan career."

Taylor was so angry that for years he would not attend Michigan football games, even though he lived in the Ann Arbor area. His wife, Tina, finally convinced him that it made no sense for him to cut himself off from his university and his favorite sport. He has been a postgame analyst the past four seasons on Ann Arbor's WTKA radio following broadcasts of Michigan games.

He and Tina married in 1993, and they live in Ypsilanti Township. They have one son, Jahmil, who was born in 2000. Taylor works as a salesman for Detroit Building Supply.

Time has mellowed Taylor, who finished his Michigan career with the third-lowest career interception percentage (2.55) in school history. "I had a lot of good times; I had a lot of bad times," he said. "Overall, I can never change the experience I went through, but it made me a stronger person. And I know people will accept me for who I am."

Where Have You Gone?

WALLY TENINGA

Wally Teninga appreciates Michigan football history and tradition as much as any former or current player, he says, because he was fortunate to have participated in some of the Wolverines' most memorable games.

Teninga, an Illinois native, was a freshman on Fritz Crisler's 1945 Michigan team that was the first to employ a two-platoon system for a game against powerhouse Army in New York's Yankee Stadium. He also played on Crisler's last Michigan team—the 1947 "Mad Magicians"—and Bennie Oosterbaan's first two teams. All three of those teams won or shared Big Ten championships, and two earned national titles. He also played in the 1948 Rose Bowl.

"To have played for both Fritz and Bennie, no one in the history of Michigan football, to my knowledge, has been luckier than me," Teninga said. "Each had their individual approaches to the great game of football, but they always shared the same objective: to play the game in the Michigan tradition."

In the case of Crisler, one of the game's greatest innovators, that often meant forging a new aspect of the tradition. Crisler is best known for inventing Michigan's signature winged helmet, but he also was the first to recognize the flexibility of college football's free substitution rule.

WALLY TENINGA
Michigan letterman: 1945, 1947-1949

Position: Halfback **Number:** 42
Hometown: Chicago, Illinois

Career rushing: 148 carries, 564 yards, 13 TDs
Career punting: Averaged 11.6 yards per return and 36.4 yards per punt

In an era when most starters remained on the field the entire game, Crisler created separate offensive and defensive units. The move made sense because it kept players rested and it allowed Michigan, particularly in 1947 and 1948, to take advantage of a wealth of talented players.

But in 1945, Crisler employed the two-platoon system against Army because he believed it gave his young Wolverines, most of whom were 17 and 18 years old, the best chance to defeat a superb Cadet team led by Glenn Davis and Doc Blanchard. "Fritz knew that he had to employ numbers rather than experience," Teninga recalled. "I fully believe the ingenuity of Crisler was the reason Michigan performed credibly. This is not to say any of us were satisfied keeping that game close. Rather, each of us felt that if he had played better, we had the tools to defeat that Army juggernaut."

Teninga recalls that as the Wolverines boarded busses outside Yost Fieldhouse to begin that road trip, Crisler went from player to player, asking: "Is there anyone here who does not believe that we can achieve victory over Army on Saturday?" That Army team, considered by many to be the finest ever produced by West Point, received much national publicity, so Michigan players understood the significant challenge they faced. Some Wolverines tried to devise slogans around which they could rally their teammates. Teninga offered: "Speed is what we need." He challenged defensive end Len Ford to come up something better, and Ford did: "Here comes the blitz from Fritz!"

Before a packed house of 70,000 spectators, Army built a 14-0 first-half lead on touchdowns by Davis and Blanchard. After the second touchdown, Teninga hauled in the kickoff, followed his blocking down the right sideline and eventually had just one Cadet to beat. Unfortunately for Teninga, the Army player was Blanchard. Recognizing that the two were on a collision course, Teninga lowered his shoulder, hoping to bull for extra yardage. But Blanchard hit Teninga "like a ton of dynamite." The blow knocked the young Wolverine out of bounds at midfield and sent the ball sailing into the second tier of seats. As Teninga struggled to get to his feet along the Michigan sideline, he announced to Oosterbaan: "Coach, I bet Blanchard felt that one!" He laughs now at that suggestion. "You may believe now that Blanchard was hardly fazed by the impact," he said. "As a matter of fact, I don't believe he lost his feet, I saw him through some rather dizzy eyes dusting himself off."

Teninga's return set up Michigan's first score, and he played a key role in it. On fourth down from the Army 9-yard line, Teninga fired a pass that glanced off the helmet of an Army defender into the hands of a surprised Art Renner, the Wolverines' right end. That was all the offense Michigan could muster that afternoon, and the Cadets added two fourth-quarter touchdowns for a 28-7 win. Reporters covering the game were impressed with Michigan's hustle and refusal to quit. One Midwest sportswriter later suggested that the Wolverines' performance, even in defeat, had upheld the Big Ten's prestige that season.

Though the war was over by then, Teninga expected to be drafted the following February when he turned 18. Instead, he enlisted in the army and served 18 months. Discharged right before the start of the 1947 season, Teninga returned to school in time to play football. He officially was listed as the backup to star left halfback Bob Chappuis, but Crisler appreciated the fact that he could play any one of the four positions in Michigan's single-wing backfield.

Teninga's versatility continued to pay dividends for the Wolverines in 1948 and again in 1949. He shared right halfback duties both seasons. He averaged 41.5 yards a punt to lead the '48 national champions. In 1949, he scored the game-winning touchdown in a stunning 14-7 upset of third-ranked Minnesota and threw a 15-yard pass to Koceski for Michigan's only touchdown in a 7-7 tie with Ohio State. He was the defensive hero in Michigan's 13-0 win at Illinois that season, forcing a fumble and recovering it, and making a touchdown-saving tackle in the open field. He also blasted a 69-yard punt in that game.

After graduating in 1950 with a degree in economics, Teninga returned to the Chicago area to join his father's real estate business. He specialized in commercial real estate. One of the company's clients was the S.S. Kresge Co., which hired him in 1954 as a real estate representative in the Detroit area. He moved in 1958 to Los Angeles, where he helped the company secure sites for its stores. While in California, Teninga moved into the company's retailing end, and he eventually became the Western Region manager. He returned to the Detroit area in the early 1960s as director of corporate growth, in charge of developing Kmart stores. He was promoted in 1971 to vice-chairman and chief financial and development officer for Kmart. That same year, he obtained a master's degree in business administration from Michigan State. He retired from Kmart in 1979.

Teninga moved back to Chicago, where he started and ran The Warehouse Club from 1980-90. He also served on several area boards of directors. He now lives in Florida with his wife, Nancy, whom he met in 1945 in Ann Arbor. The couple has two grown children, a son and a daughter.

Crisler was a man of few words—his players learned to gauge his mood by studying his facial expressions and body language—so a compliment from the head coach was meaningful. Teninga was a backup in 1947, but Crisler so appreciated his versatility that he offered this glowing assessment of the player to a local newspaper: "There is no kid on this team whose value means any more to Michigan than Teninga. No matter who gets hurt, it is comforting to the coach to know Wally is around."

BOB TIMBERLAKE

Bob Timberlake is regarded as one of the great quarterbacks in Michigan history. A three-year starter, he led the Wolverines to Big Ten and Rose Bowl championships in 1964, his senior season. He was the Big Ten's most valuable player that year. He is one of four players in program history to be honored as a first-team All-American both for his football and academic achievements.

Ironically, the game Timberlake remembers most is the one in which he didn't play. Sidelined because of a shoulder injury, Timberlake watched as eventual Heisman Trophy winner Roger Staubach led Navy to a 26-13 win at Michigan Stadium in 1963. "He was the best quarterback I ever saw," Timberlake said. "He was tremendously talented, and he was an amazingly good scrambler. On one play, he was turned around in the pocket, but he spun and fired a blind pass that was right on target. He was one of a kind, and it would have been fun to play against him."

A native of Franklin, Ohio, Timberlake chose Michigan because he believed he would be challenged by the university's high academic standards and because he respected Michigan head coach Bump Elliott.

The 6-4 Timberlake was valued for his versatility: He also played defensive back and running back, and he handled all of the team's place-kicking. "There were some ridiculous rules for substitutions in those

BOB TIMBERLAKE
Michigan letterman: 1962-1964

Position: Quarterback **Number:** 28
Hometown: Franklin, Ohio

All-American, 1964. Big Ten MVP, 1964.
Career passing: 133 of 269 for 1,656 yards, 8 TDs, 12 interceptions
Career rushing: 328 carries, 967 yards, 10 TDs **Top game:** 145 yards
and 1 TD passing; 18 carries for 113 yards and 2 TDs vs. Purdue, 1964

days, so you learned to go both ways," he said. "I played where I was needed, but I didn't really have the right size or skills to play halfback."

His first two seasons as starter were not memorable in terms of record. The 1962 team finished 2-7 overall and last in the Big Ten. The 1963 team finished 3-4-2 and tied for fifth in the conference. But those struggles forged a championship team that earned Michigan its first trip to the Rose Bowl since 1950. Timberlake accumulated 1,381 yards of total offense that season—then the second highest total in school history. He also scored 80 points himself, on eight touchdowns, four field goals and 20 extra points.

Timberlake remembers bits and pieces of each game that season. On a critical third-and-long play against Illinois, he looked to the sideline to get a signal from Elliott for the next play and was stunned that his head coach had turned his back on him. Timberlake called for a roll-out pass, completed it for a first down, and the Wolverines went on to post a 21-6 win. In a 10-0 win at Ohio State on a bitterly cold November day, he completed a 15-yard pass to Jim Detwiler for the game's only touchdown.

"We had a lot of good offensive games, but the strength of our team was the defense," he said. "That Ohio State game was another testimony to our defense. One of the things that made that Ohio State win even sweeter was the fact that 14 of our starters were guys from Ohio."

Though Michigan teams have been to the Rose Bowl many times the past four decades, the '64 team's trip to Pasadena was just the fourth in school history. "Remember, there weren't as many bowl games then as there are now, and that was the only game a Big Ten team could go to, so it was feast or famine," he said. "To be able to go was quite an honor. No one on our team was used to playing in front of a national TV audience, so it was a big step up, and we felt a great deal of pressure."

The Wolverines' jitters didn't last long. After spotting Oregon State a 7-0 lead in the second quarter, they roared back to post a 34-7 triumph. Timberlake completed seven of his 10 pass attempts for 77 yards, and he ran 12 times for 57 yards. He accounted for 10 of his team's points on a 24-yard touchdown run, two extra points and a two-point conversion run.

Timberlake was selected by the New York Giants in the third round of the 1965 Draft. He played one season for the Giants as a quarterback and a kicker and on special teams, but he was cut the following season. He was devastated, but he says he realizes now that it was a blessing. He has not had the knee and hip injuries that have plagued many of his former teammates who had longer professional careers. Now, at age 60, he can jog, bike and cross-country ski without pain.

Timberlake, who'd earned a degree in sociology from Michigan, was accepted into the Princeton Theological Seminary during his season with the Giants. He moved to Wisconsin after his graduation, and he served as a Presbyterian minister for nine years before moving into hospital administration. He has tutored grade- and middle-school students in math and taught a GED math class to older students for years. Now semi-retired, he is teaching a class entitled "Decent and Affordable Housing" in the Marquette University department of civil and environmental engineering this fall. He planned to base much of the course on his experiences helping to build houses for Habitat for Humanity in the Milwaukee area. "Marquette has a very strong moral base, and it is very intent on making a change in the world," he explained. "So, if I teach a course on housing, there has to be a component in it on social justice."

Timberlake's wife, Bobbi, directs the service learning program at Marquette University. The program matches as many as 900 students each semester with school- and community-based volunteer organizations. The Timberlakes have two children: Karen, a Harvard Law School graduate; and Jeff, an urban sociology professor at the University of Cincinnati.

Timberlake returned to Ann Arbor last fall for the 100th Michigan-Ohio State game, and he participated in pregame ceremonies with hundreds of other former Michigan players. The experience was an unforgettable one, he said, and he plans to be back at his alma mater this fall for the 40th reunion of the '64 team.

"I enjoyed seeing so many of my former teammates," he said. "A high percentage of them graduated, and an amazing number of them entered professional careers. I am very proud of that. We truly were student-athletes."

DICK VIDMER

If Dick Vidmer could live his life over, he would not change a thing. He is satisfied with his Michigan football career, but he knows he might have had a most memorable one had he not suffered a serious leg injury during his freshman season. Each day, rather than fret about what he does not have, he gives thanks for the gifts he has received. Most important of all, he does not spend his days despairing over the multiple sclerosis that ravaged his nervous system, put him in a wheelchair, and eventually left him a quadriplegic.

"If I could change it back, I wouldn't," the 59-year-old Vidmer said of his life. "I don't think I could have learned so many important lessons without having experienced this. I don't go to doctors or take medicine. I am not certain what progress has been made in the search for a cure (for MS). I hope some day one is found. (But) it is not for me."

Vidmer's road to self-discovery began more than two decades after he finished his playing career at Michigan. He had begun to detect early symptoms of MS—in which the body's own immune system attacks the insulating material surrounding the nerves that carry signals to and from various body parts—in the late 1970s, and he was diagnosed with the disease in 1983.

He decided to fight the disease for all his worth, and he promised his wife that he would never be confined to a wheelchair. He exercised

DICK VIDMER
Michigan letterman: 1945, 1965-1967

Position: Quarterback **Number:** 27
Hometown: Greensburg, Pennsylvania

Academic All-American, 1966
Career passing: 181 of 367, 2,400 yards, 11 TDs
Top game: 15 of 19, 210 yards, 3 TDs vs. Minnesota, 1966

harder than ever. He gave up eating meat and cheese. He took the latest drugs. He explored alternative forms of therapy such as acupuncture and massage. But, no matter what he tried, the disease slowly broke him down until he could no longer stand or dress himself.

Vidmer had reached a crossroads. More than once, he sat at his dining room table contemplating suicide, believing it was the only way out of a horrible situation. Gradually, however, he let go of his ego, accepted what was happening to him, and began to experience an inner peace and an understanding about life that he never could have imagined before.

"This disease has been a gift," Vidmer said. "It is the best thing that ever happened to me. It gave me an opportunity over a period of time to change my life's focus by the way that I experience and interpret the world outside and inside. It is something I really did not have the incentive to do before this disease. I think I have become much more spiritual. I never spent 10 seconds exploring what that word means and how you move into other realms of awareness. Although my physical body has been devastated in terms of what it can do, the key things, by some stroke of the miraculous, have been undamaged. My mind is clear. I am not in pain. I can hear and see and breathe. All the things I have to do, I can do. When I see trees, the world looks more beautiful to me. I didn't see that before."

Vidmer, from Greensburg, Pennsylvania, was one of the finest prep quarterbacks ever produced by his state. He was a marvelous athlete who was equally adept at running and passing, and he was such an outstanding student that every Ivy League school recruited him. He was particularly impressed by Harvard, and he told his father he planned to go there. However, he changed his mind after a visit to the Cambridge, Massachusetts, college. He was escorted on his campus visit by a bearded, long-haired student who told Vidmer that if was looking to play bigtime football, he should go to some other school. "The more I thought about it, I realized I couldn't go to a place like that and be content with missing a chance to play football at the highest level," he said. The student, who hailed from Pittsburgh, suggested that Vidmer consider Michigan.

Vidmer has three degrees from Michigan: a bachelor's in economics; a master's in international relations; and a Ph.D. in political science and Soviet area studies. He was a Big Ten scholar-athlete and an academic All-American. He taught at the University of Virginia, and later served as an advisor in Washington to Pennsylvania congressman Don Bailey, a former Michigan teammate. He went on to have his own public service career, as a Westmoreland (Pennsylvania) county commissioner, before his battle with MS forced him to retire in 1999.

As a freshman at Michigan, Vidmer quickly established himself in 1964 as the heir apparent at quarterback to Bob Timberlake, who led the Wolverines to the Big Ten championship that season. But during a practice scrimmage, Vidmer's spikes stuck in the ground as he attempted to spin away from a tackle, and the force of contact tore ankle ligaments and broke one of the bones in his lower leg. In the three seasons that followed, Vidmer struggled to regain his previous form. "I was never able to move around like I could before," he said. "It made a difference in my effectiveness. I was not as formidable a player as I once was." In 1965 and 1967, he was in and out of the starting lineup. As the full-time starter in 1966, he led Michigan to a 6-4 finish and a 4-3 Big Ten record.

He set a Michigan single-game record of 47 pass attempts in 1966 during a 20-7 loss at Michigan State. The record has since been surpassed twice. He averaged 111 yards passing a game in his career, eighth best in school history. He threw for 150 or more yards in a game eight times. In his best statistical game, he was 12-of-18 passing for 258 yards in 41-0 win against Oregon State in 1966.

Vidmer says he remembers both the bad and good moments of his career. He threw an interception against Illinois that was returned 98 yards for a touchdown. It is still the longest interception return by an opponent in school history. Two weeks earlier in a 49-0 homecoming win against Minnesota, he completed 15 consecutive pass attempts. "Everything just seemed to click for me in that (Minnesota) game," he said.

Vidmer remains devoted to his alma mater, and it is quickly evident in any conversation that he remains passionate about Michigan football. He still analyzes tape of every game, and he returns to Ann Arbor once each season to attend a game. In 2003, he watched the Wolverines pound Notre Dame, 38-0.

Even when he talks about MS, his football background is apparent.

"One thing I am thankful for is that the disease gave me a chance to adjust incrementally over the years," he said. "It would have been bad if this had happened in one fell swoop, but I got the chance to buckle it up. My greatest fear as I battled this thing was that I couldn't take it. I was absolutely convinced I could beat this thing down with my force of will and discipline. I was naïve, but I believed it. When it would not bend to my will, I started thinking differently and understanding things differently."

When another former Wolverine, Terry Barr, was asked to speak to the Michigan team before its 1995 season opener against Virginia, he called Vidmer for advice. Vidmer suggested to Barr that he speak from his own life experiences.

Vidmer has since thought many times about what he might say to the team if he ever got the opportunity. "I would tell them there is no reason to keep anything in and no reason to fear," he said. "This is their chance, and they will never have it again. They should let it all hang out and savor the moment, because it will not be around much."

TRIPP WELBORNE

Tripp Welborne smiles knowingly when someone suggests he was born 10 years too early to take full advantage of his marvelous athletic ability. Welborne was so dominant as a high school player that recruiting analysts ranked him as the nation's top prospect *both* as a wide receiver and as a defensive back, and at points during his Michigan career he played one position or the other. But he never played both during the same season, as future Heisman Trophy Charles Woodson would for the Wolverines during the 1997 national championship season.

"At that time, Michigan coaches were not receptive to an idea like that," Welborne said. "(Coach) Bo (Schembechler) told me that if I wanted to play both ways, I should go to Holy Cross and be another Gordie Lockbaum (the two-way Crusaders star who was third in the Heisman Trophy balloting in 1987). That made me laugh."

Welborne, a native of Greensboro, North Carolina, was determined to play on offense when he got to Michigan, and in '87 he joined a receiving corps that included John Kolesar, Chris Calloway, Greg McMurtry and two excellent tight ends. It was a strong group, but with quarterback Jim Harbaugh gone, the Wolverines relied more on running than passing. Welborne caught just two passes his freshmen season, but he made several open-field tackles because Michigan's young quarter-

TRIPP WELBORNE
Michigan letterman: 1987-1990

Position: Defensive back **Number:** 3
Hometown: Greensboro, North Carolina

All-American, 1989-90
Career defense: 227 tackles, 30 pass breakups, 8 interceptions
Career punt returns: 67 for 773 yards

backs threw a lot of interceptions, and he demonstrated his defensive skills because he played on all special teams.

Michigan defensive coaches began to lobby hard to get him, but he did not want to leave the offense. As a compromise, Welborne suggested to Schembechler that he be allowed to play both on offense and defense, as Woodson would do a decade later. The head coach wasn't fond of the idea, but he allowed Welborne to divide his practice time in the spring of 1988 between offense and defense.

"I didn't really want to play defense, but I have a lot of pride, so I did my best," Welborne said. "Once I got on defense, I made some plays over there that hadn't been made in a while. The lobbying for the defense won out."

When the '88 season began, Welborne was officially on defense, and he became a sort of wild card because he could play any position in the secondary. With his speed, he could cover any receiver man for man, and he had the size to make his presence felt as a run-stopper and blitzer. He recorded 238 tackles and intercepted nine passes in three seasons on defense. He was able to demonstrate his offensive skills on special teams. He returned 67 punts in four seasons for 773 yards, and in 1990 he set a single-season school record with 455 yards in punt returns. He was a consensus All-America selection in 1989 and 1990.

In two respects, it is amazing that Welborne ever ended up at Michigan. He was certain he was not a cold weather kind of guy. "I was much more aligned with the Florida boys in terms of playing … in cut-off jerseys," he said. "I was used to nice weather." He also abhorred artificial turf, saying he preferred grass stains to rug burns. "I never liked turf," he said. "I still don't."

That's why Michigan was not at the top of Welborne's recruiting list when he narrowed his college choices in 1987. He liked Florida State and UCLA, both of which played in warm weather and on grass. But he wasn't prepared to dismiss Michigan from consideration. The school's engineering program was attractive, as was the Wolverines' storied football tradition. Those things were enough to convince him to visit Ann Arbor.

What he saw during his visit changed his mind about cold weather. As he entered quiet, snow-covered Michigan Stadium, he noticed a set of footprints leading out of the tunnel to the middle of the field. There, someone had traced a huge block "M" in the snow. "I thought: 'If someone was crazy enough to do that, this place might just work for me,'" Welborne recalled. "I recognized right then that the people here are definitely excited and into their football. When I got back home, I decided that was the place I needed to go. The cream rose to the top."

However, Welborne will never have anything good to say about artificial turf, which he saw for the first time at Michigan and played on for four seasons. As he had suspected, the feel of football on turf was different: While the game was noticeably faster, the fake stuff didn't give the way grass does. He would experience that the hard way—twice—during his career. "The first time I played on it, I thought: 'Man, you need to tear this up,'" he said. "The last game I played in Michigan Stadium was the last game (on carpet). The next year, they put in grass."

That was one year too late for Welborne, whose college career came to a painful end on that turf. As he neared the out-of-bounds marker on a punt return along the visitor's sideline during the 1990 home finale against Minnesota, Welborne attempted to cut back toward the field to gain some extra yards. As he did, someone grabbed his shoulder pad and spun him around. His right leg caught in the turf, causing extensive ligament and cartilage damage to his knee. "What's amazing about it is that was the very first play I ever missed in my entire career at Michigan," he said. "You would have figured I would have gone out for at least one play at some point, but I never did. I went from iron man to being injury-prone on one play."

Drafted by the Minnesota Vikings, Welborne spent the entire 1991 season rehabbing his injured knee. When he returned to action in 1992, his professional career lasted eight games. Against Detroit at the Metrodome in Minneapolis, Welborne landed awkwardly on his left leg after hurdling an opposing blocker and was pushed just as he came down. His left knee buckled. He had torn the anterior cruciate ligament. The injury was not as severe as the one he'd suffered at Michigan, so he tried to come back the following season, but he injured the same knee again. That ended his football career.

After he left football, Welborne started Bornwell, Inc., an organization that provides scholarships and seminars for young people. He eventually moved into financial services, working for Wachovia brokerage and for the Bank of America as a risk manager. He recently returned to Minneapolis to take a job with Target Financial Services. "I told the people there I hope my stay lasts longer than the 2 1/2 years I was with the Vikings," he said. He and his wife, Christy, have been married for five years. The couple has one daughter, Dylan, who is two years old.

Though he can remember every play from every game he played in since he was 10 years old, Welborne says games don't stand out to him because of his individual achievements. He remembers the games that were important to his teams. He vividly recalls back-to-back losses to Notre Dame and Miami (Florida) to start the 1988 season, as much for pain of those defeats as for the way the Wolverines bounced back to win the Big Ten championship and the Rose Bowl. "What you learn real quick is that you can work hard and still not win," he said. "Your hard work gives you the opportunity to win, but the guys on the other team are working just as hard as you."

Where Have You Gone?

THOMAS
WILCHER

After two seasons of battling ankle and knee injuries, junior Thomas Wilcher finally broke loose in the second nonconference game of the 1985 season at South Carolina. In four career games in three seasons to that point, including the opener against Notre Dame the previous weekend, Wilcher had carried eight times for a total of 24 yards. But against the Gamecocks, Wilcher ran 16 times for 104 yards and his first career touchdown.

His first carry of the game wasn't much of a harbinger of the good things to come. In fact, judging by that first carry, the sellout Williams-Brice Stadium crowd must have been wondering whether Wilcher—forget about his career—would ever get off the ground.

Wilcher took that first handoff, followed his offensive linemen as they slanted to the left, and then cut back into what he hoped would be an opening in the heart of the South Carolina defense. Instead, as he turned to make his cut, he slammed into a linebacker. The force of the collision sent Wilcher's helmet sailing through the air, which prompted a noticeable gasp and then a loud roar for the defense from the partisan crowd. His teammates still like to tease him about that hit—"It's something everyone laughs about," he said—but Wilcher insists it was not as brutal as it looked. He says he was wearing his helmet too loosely.

THOMAS WILCHER
Michigan letterman: 1985-1986

Position: Tailback **Number:** 27
Hometown: Detroit, Michigan

Career rushing: 166 carries, 758 yards, 8 TDs
Top game: 16 carries, 104 yards, 1 TD at South Carolina, 1985

But he learned from the experience. The Wolverines ran the same play on second down, and this time Wilcher cut up rather than back. He blew by the defender who had knocked off his helmet, and by the time he was tackled, he'd gained close to 30 yards. That run sparked Michigan's first scoring drive, and the Wolverines went on to post a 34-3 victory.

It was the sort of game Wilcher and Michigan fans had imagined when he was recruited out of Detroit Central High School. There wasn't anything particularly fancy about his running style: He hit the hole quickly, made shallow cuts and then let his sprinter's speed do the rest. "We had a lot of running backs, and each guy had his own strength," Wilcher said. "We had all kind of different talent, and the coaches tried to use them as best they could. The key to playing was to try to make certain your strength fit one of the roles in the offense."

Wilcher, a football and track star in high school, considered Tennessee, Southern Cal and Michigan. He liked Tennessee's tradition in both football and track, and he liked USC's history of producing Heisman Trophy winners at tailback. He admired Michigan's athletic tradition, too, and his mother especially liked Coach Bo Schembechler. That clinched the decision for Wilcher.

But, while he could outrun just about anyone in high school (he was a national record holder in every hurdle event), injuries overtook him almost from the minute he got to Michigan. He injured his right ankle twice his freshman season, once in training camp and then again midway through the season when a linebacker fell on the back of his leg. After the second injury, he would always need to have his ankle heavily taped. "The trainers used to go through two rolls of tape on me every day before practice," he said. Even that precaution was not a guarantee against trouble. He endured several ankle sprains throughout his career.

He even had injury problems in track. During an outdoor meet against Michigan State the spring of his freshman year, Wilcher landed sideways at the end of a long jump, tearing the lateral collateral ligament in his right knee. The knee and ankle injuries limited him to three games during his first two seasons. "I never did long jump again," he said. "Bo told (Michigan track coach) Jack Harvey that I had to quit it. It's too bad, because that had been one of my strongest events in high school."

Wilcher alternated at the tailback spot with Jamie Morris for much of his senior season, but he started the Big Ten opener at Wisconsin and again the following weekend against Michigan State. The Wisconsin game was particularly memorable, Wilcher says, because, with a number of the other tailbacks hurt, he got most of the carries. He ran 22 times for 74 yards and two touchdowns. His longest run of the game was nine yards. "I was dead tired after that one was over," he said. "We were so used to alternating, but I had to play the whole game. No breaks, no nothing. And that was one of the toughest games we played all season. Of all the teams we used to play, Wisconsin always hit the hardest. They were always very tough and aggressive."

San Diego selected Wilcher in the ninth round of the 1987 NFL Draft. The Chargers wanted him primarily as a defensive back, but he says team officials promised him he would get a shot at running back. That never happened, and he did not make the team's final cut. Coaches offered to let him remain on the practice squad so he could learn more about playing in the secondary, but he refused and the Chargers released him. Other teams contacted him about playing, but they, too, wanted him as a defensive back. He returned to school to complete his degree.

Once back in Ann Arbor, he got the opportunity to coach the junior varsity football team and the varsity track sprinters at Huron High School. Other coaches at the school were so impressed with the job he did that they suggested he become a teacher. With a concentration of courses in physical education and social science, Wilcher earned a teaching certificate in 1989.

He did his student teaching at Detroit Cass Technical High School. Two of his former coaches at Central, Dave Sneed and Woody Thomas, pushed him to return to the Detroit Public Schools to teach and coach. He has taught physical education, health and swimming and has been the head track coach at Cass Tech for 13 years. He also is now the school's head football coach.

Wilcher has been married to Crystal Dawn Young-Wilcher for 11 years. The couple has three children: a son, Kishon, 10; and two daughters, Kaila, 9, and Keirsten, 5. The family lives in Detroit.

If Wilcher has one regret about his football career, it is that he did not consider opportunities to play defensive back, particularly with the Chargers. "My hindsight is, maybe I didn't see my potential as a defensive back," he said. "I didn't do it at Michigan, though I played on all the special teams. I guess it was just me being stubborn."

Where Have You Gone?

ALBERT WISTERT

A lbert Wistert has, during the course of his lifetime, wound up in all kinds of exclusive company.

He is the youngest of Michigan's three famed Wistert brothers. Each brother played the same tackle positions on offense and defense, earned first-team All-America honors and wore the same jersey number, 11. No other brother combination in the history of college football has achieved anything like that.

He also is one of only three players in American football history to have jersey numbers retired by both their college and professional teams. The brothers' number is one of five retired by Michigan. The Philadelphia Eagles retired Wistert's number, 70, in 1951, when he retired after a nine-year All-Pro career. The other two players who share that distinction? Dick Butkus and Johnny Unitas.

"That's pretty exclusive company, and I'm very proud to be in it," Wistert said. "But I am more proud of what my brothers and I accomplished at Michigan. It is a thrilling, thrilling thing to have been a part of that. Imagine how great it is for the three of us to go to school at Michigan, then to be on the football team, and then to be All-Americans. It's so fabulous, even to this day it's exciting to think about."

ALBERT WISTERT
Michigan letterman: 1940-1942

Position: Tackle **Number:** 11
Hometown: Chicago, Illinois

All-American, 1942

The Wistert brothers grew up on Chicago's north side. Their father, a police officer, was shot when Albert was five, and died of complications from the wound a year later. Their mother would not allow the boys to play high school football because she could not afford to take them to a doctor if they were injured. Still, the Wisterts were always in excellent physical condition, because their father taught them to be physical culturists. Wistert, who still exercises each day, recalls that his father used to do chin-ups "with me hanging on his belt."

The oldest Wistert brother, Francis, nicknamed Whitey, played at Michigan from 1931-33. His last two teams won Big Ten and national championships. At age 12, Albert Wistert got a chance to see his older brother play in his home town in 1933, when Michigan won 28-0 at the University of Chicago. It was a memorable afternoon for the youngest Wistert, who decided that day he would follow his brother to Michigan. He was impressed by the Chicago halfback, Jay Berwanger, who two years later would become the first player to win the Heisman Trophy. One of the first Michigan players to greet young Albert Wistert in the locker room after the game was a future U.S. president, Gerald Ford. A couple of years later, Francis Wistert took his brother to Wrigley Field to watch the Chicago Bears play the New York Giants for the National Football League championship. Albert Wistert decided that afternoon he would also play professional football. "I was lucky," he said. "I realized both of my dreams."

Albert Wistert enrolled at Michigan in 1938 and would have played as a sophomore in 1939 had he not broken his ankle in practice before the season opener. He sat out that season as a redshirt player. He says the extra year off better prepared him to play because he'd had no high school experience. He was the only sophomore in the starting lineup in 1940, which was Tom Harmon's senior season. "I was pretty green in terms of what I knew about football, but I had all seniors around me, so that was a big help."

Wistert says he was never bold enough to ask for the No. 11 jersey his older brother had worn, but Michigan equipment manager Henry Hatch had saved it for him. When Wistert went to the equipment room to pick up his game uniform for picture-taking day in 1940, Hatch reach under the counter and pulled out No. 11. Wistert began to cry. "I never needed a pep talk after that," he said. "Every time I put on that jersey, that was all I needed."

Wistert began to build a reputation for himself during a 14-0 win against Pennsylvania in late October at Michigan Stadium. At breakfast that morning, Harmon pulled Wistert aside and told him that if he hoped to become an All-American like his older brother, that was the day to have a good game. With the press box full of national sportswriters, Wistert put on such a show that he upstaged Harmon. Newspaper headlines the following morning read: "Wistert and Harmon beat Quakers." "I could do nothing wrong that day," he recalled. "Many times I would hear over the P.A. system: 'Wistert makes another tackle.'"

Two weeks later, the Wolverines would suffer their only loss of the season, 7-6 at Minnesota. It would be the start of a bad trend for the youngest Wistert: He never beat the Golden Gophers in three tries. Neither of his brothers ever lost to Minnesota. "That loss in 1940 still rankles in my heart," he said. "Minnesota wound up winning the national championship that season because they beat us. I wanted to win a national championship because Whitey had won one, but I never did. I wanted to be an All-American like he was. That worked out for me."

Wistert also played in one of the most memorable games in the Michigan-Notre Dame series, in 1942 in South Bend, Indiana. The Wolverines trailed by a point at halftime, and as they headed off the field into the locker room, some Notre Dame fans taunted them, saying: "Better luck next year!" The insults motivated Wistert and the team's other seniors. Michigan scored three touchdowns in the second half to post a 32-20 win.

Michigan coach Fritz Crisler devised a tackle-around play during the 1941 season to take advantage of the speedy Wistert on the far end of the Wolverines' unbalanced line. He carried the ball just once that season, for seven yards in a game at Northwestern, but he broke his nose and left wrist on the play. The wrist injury later prompted army doctors to reject him for military service because X-rays indicated he might have tuberculosis in the bone.

Instead of going into the army, Wistert played professional football. He spent nine All-Pro seasons in Philadelphia, during which he helped the Eagles win NFL championships in 1948 and 1949. He was the team captain during his final five seasons. Looking to earn some extra income, Wistert also coached area high school teams while he played in Philadelphia. He would practice with the Eagles in the morning, coach his own team in the afternoon, and then get back in time for the Eagles' evening meetings. One of his teams, Riverside High School, won the New Jersey state championship while he was head coach.

After earning a degree in history from Michigan and a degree in education from Temple, Wistert briefly considered teaching and coaching as a career, but he instead found his calling in the life insurance business. He worked as a salesman and executive for Bankers Life Nebraska for 40 years, first in Philadelphia, then in Detroit and finally in southern California. He says he was a million-dollar producer for the company.

The 84-year-old Wistert and his high school sweetheart, Ellie, recently celebrated their 61st wedding anniversary. The couple has three daughters: Pamela, Dianna, and Kathy.

The Wisterts bought a five-acre piece of property in Grants Pass, Oregon, in 1991 so Kathy could raise her nine horses. Wistert didn't know it at the time, but that move put him into more exclusive company. Grants Pass was the hometown of Willie Heston, the All-America running back who starred for Fielding H. Yost's first four Michigan teams. "They just inducted (Heston) into their Hall of Fame out here, and I did that job for them," Wistert said. "They don't even realize what a great player he was."

ALVIN WISTERT

Everywhere Alvin Wistert went, it seemed, he was mistaken for one of his famous brothers, Francis or Albert. He was constantly introduced as the All-American from Michigan, and he had to politely explain that he wasn't the person they thought, that he'd never been to college.

As proud as he was of his brothers and their accomplishments at Michigan—both had been All-America tackles—he was tired of being asked about and compared to them, particularly because he had not done what they had. His frustration came to head in 1945, when word spread around the Navy troop ship carrying his company of marines to the south Pacific that one of the famous Wistert brothers was on board. He was approached by a navy lieutenant, who shook his hand enthusiastically and announced to everyone that he'd seen Wistert play for the Philadelphia Eagles against the New York Giants in Yankee Stadium. Wistert informed the officer that he'd seen his brother, not him, and that he'd never been to college. The stunned lieutenant yanked back his hand, quickly turned and walked away from the dumbfounded Wistert.

"He acted as if I was a nothing, that he should never have shaken my hand," Wistert said. "I was so offended by his behavior that I sat down that night and wrote my younger brother (Albert). I told him I was

ALVIN WISTERT
Michigan letterman: 1947-1949

Position: Tackle **Number:** 11
Hometown: Chicago, Illinois

All-American, 1948-49. Captain, 1949.

mighty proud of what he and Whitey had accomplished, but that I was sick and tired of the comparisons. I told him that when I got out of the marines, I was going to come back to school and try to be somebody. I did just that."

The Wistert brothers, from Chicago, were four years apart in age. Francis, the oldest and nicknamed Whitey, had starred for Michigan's national championship teams of 1932 and '33, and he pitched briefly in professional baseball. Albert, the youngest, was a stalwart on Fritz Crisler's teams of the early 1940s.

Alvin, the middle brother, had considered Michigan, too, but he was more interested in athletics than academics. He dropped out of high school a month before graduation in 1935 because he expected to become a professional baseball pitcher. He was invited to the Cincinnati Reds' spring training in 1936. His dream ended that winter after he slipped on a patch of ice and injured his pitching elbow. "My baseball career was over before it ever began," he said. "I decided I'd blown my chance at a college education, so I went to work."

With the war over, Wistert got the opportunity he wanted. After he went back to work for a Massachusetts company that had hired him before the war, he learned that Boston University was offering high school equivalency tests to returning veterans. Wistert passed, was admitted to school, and played as a freshman on the Boston University football team at the age of 30. Early in the fall, he wrote to the Michigan admissions office and asked what he needed to do to transfer there for the second semester. He was told he needed a "B" average, and he got it.

He discovered that the comparisons to his brothers were only beginning. He was given the number 11 the other two had worn—it is one of five numbers retired by Michigan—and he played the same left tackle spot (next to the center) on Michigan's unbalanced offensive line. While throwing a block during practice that first spring, he heard freshman coach Wally Weber shout: "Your brother used to hit harder than that!" "I kept thinking: 'What do I have to do to live down that brother image?'" he recalled. "Wally had the needle out, thinking he was motivating me."

The comparisons finally ended in 1948, his junior season, when he was named an All-American. He was delighted, he says, because he'd achieved one of the goals he'd set for himself. All three Wisterts are enshrined in the College Football Hall of Fame. Alvin Wistert was inducted in 1981. "It is unprecedented in the history of college football that three brothers achieved all those things," he said. "It's only happened once, and it probably will never happen again."

Wistert says he is proud that the Wolverines never lost to Minnesota in the three seasons he played. His older brothers' teams had beaten the Golden Gophers twice and tied them once—never giving up a point in the process—but Albert Wistert's teams had lost all three games they'd played against Minnesota. "When I came to Ann Arbor, I vowed that over my dead body would Minnesota ever beat us," he said. "That is how strongly I felt about beating them. I wanted to avenge the three losses Albert had suffered." Defensive lineman Leo Nomellini was one of the stars of those Minnesota teams of the late 1940s, and he once told Wistert's sister that her brother was one of the toughest players he'd ever faced. "He said the coaches used to tell him: 'You think you're mean. That Wistert is so mean he slaps his mother every day before breakfast.'"

The game Wistert remembers most is one of the two the Wolverines lost during his career, 21-7 to Army in 1949. Wistert had injured his knee the week before at Stanford, but he insisted on playing against the Cadets. His strength as a defensive lineman was his lateral movement, but his knee was so heavily taped for the Army game that his movement was severely hampered. Despite his warnings the following week, Michigan players fretted about their loss to Army rather than focus on the upcoming game at Northwestern. The Wolverines lost that game, too, 21-20.

With a degree in physical education, Wistert briefly considered a career as a football coach, but he decided against it. He worked five years for Proctor & Gamble and then worked for Owens-Illinois until his retirement at age 72. He is now 88 years old.

While attending a geology lecture in Hill Auditorium his freshman year, Wistert noticed a red-headed co-ed seated several rows in front of him. He turned to a friend and announced he intended to marry the young woman one day, though he hadn't yet met her. Her name was Nancy, and they were married in 1948. She is 13 years his junior. The couple has two daughters, Beverly and Kristen. Interestingly, none of the three Wistert brothers had any sons, only daughters.

Wistert accomplished one thing at Michigan that his brothers never did: He was elected captain of the 1949 team. He was 33 years old. "I was the oldest guy on the team," he said. "The other players looked up to me, and they respected the fact that I was going through the same things they were."

ROGER ZATKOFF

R oger Zatkoff was destined to be a linebacker, whether he liked it or not.

Zatkoff wanted to be an end when he first tried out for the Hamtramck High School football team in the late 1940s. That was the same position his uncle, Sam Zatkoff, had played at the University of Illinois. He looked for opportunities in practice to try that position, but he never got one.

Then came the practice that changed the direction of his career. After one of the team's veteran linebackers was injured, the Hamtramck head coach called for a substitute. Zatkoff refused to budge. The coach pointed a finger at Zatkoff and ordered him into the lineup. Reluctantly, he began to slowly walk toward the huddle. "The next thing I knew, I had a size-nine shoe in my rear end," Zatkoff said with a hearty laugh. "Then the coach yells at me: 'When I tell you to do something, I mean run!' That's how I became a linebacker."

An awfully good one, as it turns out. He started three seasons (1950-52) for Michigan and earned All-Big Ten honors his senior season. He played six seasons in the National Football League—four for the Green Bay Packers and two for the Detroit Lions—before a knee injury ended his career. Zatkoff's prowess at the position was such that the U-

ROGER ZATKOFF
Michigan letterman: 1950-1952

Position: Linebacker **Number:** 70
Hometown: Hamtramck, Michigan

All-Big Ten, 1952

M Club of Greater Detroit eventually would name the award it presents annually to the Wolverines' top linebacker in his honor.

Zatkoff had the ideal mentality to be a linebacker. "I loved making hits," he said. "I loved hitting a guy, grinding him into the ground and hearing him grunt. I looked forward to making great hits. I loved that. My nickname in pro ball was 'Zany.' That's because everyone thought I was crazy, especially when I was running down the field on kickoffs. Everybody called me "Zany.'"

Zatkoff was anything but crazy when it came time to choose a college. One of 10 senior starters from the Hamtramck team to play college football, he tried as he considered prospective schools, to determine which ones offered him the best opportunities to play at his position. After Michigan State offered a scholarship to another all-state linebacker, he decided to go to Michigan.

It was rare for players to start at Michigan as sophomores, but Zatkoff and Lowell Perry were in the lineup for the 1950 season opener against Michigan State. The Wolverines lost 14-7, but Zatkoff played well. A week later, as Zatkoff was being taped by trainer Jim Hunt before the Dartmouth game, Michigan athletic director and former head coach Fritz Crisler wandered past. Zatkoff had never met Crisler, so Hunt introduced the two. Crisler said: "I know you … good game, by the way." He then left the room. Zatkoff, who was proud of his effort in the MSU game, had expected a more glowing compliment, so he said to Hunt: "I thought I had a heck of a game." Hunt replied: "You don't understand. That was a very high compliment from Fritz."

Zatkoff injured his left knee—the same one he later would injure as a pro—during the final home game that season, a 34-23 win against Northwestern, so he did not play in the "Snow Bowl" game the following Saturday at Ohio State. Until that time, he'd played both linebacker and offensive tackle. Because he'd been hurt while playing on offense, once he was healthy enough to return to the lineup, he never again played tackle.

He played outside linebacker for four seasons with the Packers after they selected him in the fifth round of the 1953 NFL Draft. He played the same position with the Lions. During his first season in Detroit, 1957, the Lions won their last NFL championship. He still wears his championship ring – right next to his "M" ring.

Zatkoff worked as a substitute teacher in the Detroit public schools after each season with the Packers. By the time he'd joined the Lions, he'd opened his own business in Detroit that distributed seals and gaskets.

The company, Zatkoff Seals and Packing, is now run by his children. He jokes that he works for them as a free consultant.

He married his high school sweetheart, Elaine, before his junior season at Michigan. The couple has six children and 11 grandchildren.

Zatkoff left Michigan needing just a few requirements to complete his education degree, and his former head coach, Bennie Oosterbaan, reminded him about it any time the two would meet. Zatkoff continued to take classes when he could. The fact that he did not have his degree was a bit embarrassing, even though he'd become a successful businessman. Once, he skipped a reunion of former players because he did not want to see Oosterbaan. When he finally completed his degree requirements after he finished his pro career, he made certain his former coach was one of the first people who knew about it.

As his pro career was nearing an end, Zatkoff became an involved member of the U-M Club of Greater Detroit, and he remains active. It is his way of paying the club back: When he was a Michigan student, the club paid his tuition (then $145 a year). The club recently named one of its scholarships for incoming freshmen in honor of Roger and Elaine Zatkoff.

Zatkoff wishes the club would consider renaming the linebacker award. It's not that he isn't honored. He is. But he believes the award would have more meaning to today's Michigan players if they were more familiar with the person for whom the award is named.

"I think maybe they should update the awards from time to time," he said. "You would never change the names of Yost or Oosterbaan or Schembechler. They are traditions at the school. But you need to freshen up the other awards with younger guys or someone from the coaching staff. Maybe name a lineman award for Jerry Hanlon. Even the young kids know who he is. To me, he will always be a tradition at Michigan."

Celebrate the Heroes of College Football
in These Other 2004 Releases from Sports Publishing!

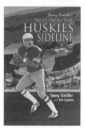

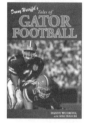